All is Calm

A Maine Christmas Reader

Other Books From Islandport Press:

Shoutin' Into The Fog
By Thomas Hanna

The Cows Are Out!
Trudy Chambers Price

Nine Mile Bridge
Helen Hamlin

Whatever It Takes
May Davidson

In Maine
By John N. Cole

Old Maine Woman
Glenna Johnson Smith

My Life in The Maine Woods
Annette Jackson

Christmas in Maine
Robert P. Tristram Coffin

These and other Maine books available at:
www.islandportpress.com

All Is Calm

A Maine Christmas Reader

Edited by
Shannon Butler

ISLANDPORT PRESS

ISLANDPORT PRESS

Islandport Press
PO Box 10
Yarmouth, Maine 04096
www.islandportpress.com
info@islandportpress.com

First Islandport Printing, 2019

ISBN: 978-1-944762-79-7
Library of Congress Card Number: 2019931597
Printed in USA.

Dean L. Lunt, Publisher
Book design, Teresa Lagrange

"*What happens to me when I cross the Piscataqua and plunge rapidly into Maine...I cannot describe it. I do not ordinarily spy a partridge in a pear tree, or three French hens, but I do have the sensation of having received a gift from a true love.*"

—E.B. White

Contents

Editor's Note

I often joke that the Maine state motto should be "progress without change." We Mainers like things the way we like them, and if progress must be made to adapt to the inevitable shifts of time, then we will always try our hardest to make sure necessary changes are minimal. The merit (or lack thereof) in having this mentality can be argued endlessly. But for better or worse, it is this attitude that has kept Maine traditions, Maine landscapes, and the Maine way of life more or less intact.

Through the process of collecting the stories of Mainers at Christmastime. I have come to realize that over the nearly two centuries the holiday has been celebrated in our fair state, we have made significant progress. Our homes are now heated and plumbed. Our Christmas dinner can be fetched at Hannaford rather than in the woods or waters. There are lights in every room to fend off the darkness that creeps in around three in the afternoon, and studded snow tires make winter travel nearly effortless.

But with this progress, has anything changed? In researching our Christmas history, it also seems obvious that for two hundred years, the month of December has resisted most modification. Our quality of life has increased, winter is no longer as difficult and perilous as it once was, but our traditions in the twelfth month have largely remained the same. Christmas trees are still cut by hand. Children still anxiously await Santa, fitfully listening for the first sign of stirring under the tree, the same as they have for decades. We decorate our homes, and prepare recipes handed down from generations past.

We light woodstoves and fireplaces, sing carols, and invite neighbors and friends to share in good cheer.

Perhaps being so tied to our landscape has helped us cling to our traditions. It's hard to accept that time is progressing when the trees, the ocean, and the mountains are steadfast. The bright stars that shine in the black, freezing night air over my grandmother's barn are the same ones my mom stared up at as a girl and the same ones my great-grandparents looked at when they crossed the snowy dooryard to tend the horses on subzero nights.

Maybe our resistance to change has come from the deep roots of community. Maine feels more like an oversized village than a state made of individual counties and municipalities. Everyone here is a cousin of someone, who is the former neighbor of someone else, who was the best friend of someone else. No Mainer is separated from another by more than a few degrees, and rarely does this show more than at Christmas. Each December, our Maine community rallies around those who are hungry, or cold, jobless, or simply without a new toy. Parties at homes, offices, and churches overflow with good cheer and neighborly affection.

It's easy to poke fun at Mainers for their stubborn nature and resistance to change, but why would we ever want to change? With abounding natural beauty, and our village of a million citizens, why would we ever feel the need to bend to the whims of time? We allow only the progress necessary to continue in this modern world but concede none of the traditions that make up our essence.

I have spent every Christmas of my life in Maine. So have my parents. So have my grandparents and so goes the family lineage about as far back as one can trace. My ancestors clearly saw the advantages and value of being in Maine long before I was born. Perhaps long enough ago that Maine is now woven into our shared DNA. Perhaps this is why I have no doubts that I will continue spending every Christmas here, surrounded by piles of snow and endless evergreens.

Even if Maine is not in my DNA, all I need to see is the vast blanket of stars over the fields on Route One north of Houlton to know that change is out of the question. If I were to change Christmas in Maine I would in turn be changing the intangible piece of myself that grounds me in a world that often feels as though it's spinning off course. Christmas in Maine is far more than the warmth of a wood fire or the sweet tang of cider—it's a shared knowledge of tradition, and community, and our natural world. The shared knowledge of that which will never change despite progress.

Merry Christmas,

Shannon Butler
Kennebunk, Maine
November 2019

A Holiday History

Maine has become the picture-perfect, snow-globe setting for a host of Christmas imagery. From idyllic, pastoral scenes on holiday cards to romantic backdrops for blossoming love in Hallmark movies, these idealized images give the notion that Maine has always been the setting for a perfect Christmas. But, the reality of biting cold, icy seas, and heavy snow actually made for a rocky start to Christmas celebrations in the northern tip of New England.

It's alleged that Maine hosted the first celebration of Christmas in the New World in 1604 (three years before the Popham Colony's known holiday ceremony) when a French fur trading ship landed on St. Croix Island, located off Calais in Passamaquoddy Bay. This little island offered the protection of being surrounded by water while the nearby mainland provided fertile farmland, bountiful game to hunt, and abundant lumber. The sailors were confident they had found the ideal place for a new settlement. Eager to establish new territory in the name of France, the men quickly began building homes and a church. To make their settlement permanent they needed more supplies. In October, fifty crew members set sail back to France while seventy men remained on St. Croix Island.

Not long after the ship had left for France, the autumn weather turned sharp and savage. Early snowstorms shocked the men who were used to mild French winters, and the river and bay that surrounded their small island became clogged with fast-moving ice jams, making crossing to the mainland impossible. The crew was stranded on a frozen island with little food, no drinking water, and very little firewood.

While no historical documents proclaim this to be an absolute truth, state lore says that in the midst of this brutal winter the men, a mix of Protestants and Catholics, held a Christmas service in the chapel they had built. They sang hymns and played games on their ice-encased island.

It is certainly possible these marooned men held a small Christmas service, but the degree of merriment on the occasion should certainly be in question. When their fellow crewmates finally returned from France in June, they found the harsh results of a diastrous winter. Thirty-five of the seventy men who stayed on the island had died.

A diet of nothing but salted meat and vegetables caused severe scurvy and left the surviving settlers with muscle pain, fatigue, loose teeth, and bruised skin. Coupled with near constant dehydration and below freezing temperatures make it difficult to imagine that first Christmas in the New World was a jovial affair.

One winter in Maine had been more than enough for the men, and they did not care to risk their lives to face another. As quickly as they had settled, they abandoned the island in 1605.

From 1605 on, Christmas remained uncelebrated in Maine as the next group of Christian settlers wanted nothing to do with the holiday.

The Puritans began founding colonies in New England in the 1630s after leaving England in search of religious freedom. In their new home, they made a point to avoid any impure traditions of the Old World that distracted from their rigorous study of faith. For the Puritans, every day was equally holy to the next and they needed no holidays.

In 1659, celebrating Christmas was banned in the Massachusetts Bay Colony with a new law stating, "whosoever shall be found observing any such day as Christmas or the like, either by forbearing of labor, feasting, or any other way . . . shall pay for every such offence five shilling as a fine."

Under pressure from the monarchy in England, the Purtians did eventually dial back their Christmas ban. However, even with Christmas celebrations allowed in the home, and the rigid Puritan faith beginning to fall out of fashion, Christmas remained a mostly obscure holiday in New England. Banks, schools, and public offices remained open on Christmas Day and business was conducted as usual. Meanwhile in England, Christmas began rising in popularity and it burst into the homes of the general public when Charles Dickens published *A Christmas Carol* in 1843 enlivening the spirit of family, feasting, and giving on the holiday.

The infectious spread of yuletide celebrations eventually made its way across the ocean to Maine where it was officially made a state holiday in 1858—thirty-eight years after statehood.

As Maine entered the Victorian era in the late 1800s, Christmas was celebrated, but only by those who could afford it. At that time, most men, women, and children worked. Women were servants and factory workers, and men worked on the water, in canneries, or in the woods. Twelve-hour days were not uncommon, even for children, whose extra income was needed to help support the family. Long work hours, hard labor, and little money to spend on anything other than basic necessities kept Christmas a sparse holiday for the majority of the population.

By the turn of the last century, Christmas was becoming profitable for many Mainers, and the culture of gift giving had gained momentum, creating a more commercialized Christmas. Department stores in the cities were booming. Newspapers from the early 1900s featured advertisements touting holiday specials on everything from clothing to shoes to jewelry. Maine was beginning to see the benefits of a growing population, and, with new labor laws in place, improvements were being made to work hours and wages. Soon the general population had more time to enjoy Christmas in some of the same ways the upper class had been for decades. Christmas was now a season, not just a day. There was a build-up to the holiday, which included shopping and decorating. It was no longer just a quiet church service on the 25th.

As Christmas continued to take off in Maine and the rest of the country, Maine became one of the top exporters of Christmas trees and wreaths in the nation, giving an extra boost to our economy. Towns, schools, and churches put on Christmas pageants and sang carols open for all to enjoy, and families began creating holiday traditions that would be passed down for generations.

Maine has witnessed Christmas morph from illegal, to mostly unnoticed, to a booming, joyous time of year. It's this joyful cheer that composes the Maine spirit and creates the backdrop for the perfect Maine Christmas.

The Glory of Maine at Yuletide

John N. Cole

1980

Three hundred and seventy-three Decembers have been swallowed by time since the first English Christmas in Maine. A lean, sparse holiday was celebrated early in the seventeenth century near the mouth of the Kennebec by Sir George Popham and the men who had sailed early that year from England to reach this corner of the New World in August.

Three hundred and seventy-three Decembers! Yet not that much has changed about this particular holiday in this most particular place. As the days of 1607 shortened so barely eight hours of diffuse sunlight separated dawn and dusk, Sir George's colonists must have spent the long nights pondering the winter still to come, even as they clung to memories of the robust and productive autumn just concluded. Today, most of Maine's one million settlers do the same. The solstice is eternal, the tilting of the earth is awesome and implacable, its orbits beyond taming, its relationships with its Brother Sun and Sister Moon as imperative now as they have been for eons. Shadows slide south as the planet's northern half turns its face away from its sun-struck brother toward the chill dark. We are, it sometimes seems, in danger of losing our star altogether as winter compresses sunlight's span.

Then, just when the days seem darkest, comes Christmas—an event most gratefully welcomed in this northern latitude. It is our assurance that the sun's restoration has begun. Sir George's men— the forty-five of the original one hundred who survived illness and maintained their determination to stay—were mariners. They knew the rhythms of the spheres; they navigated by the stars. They understood the astronomical significance of their Church of England holiday; they were not that far removed in time from the sun's calibrator at Stonehenge nor the Druid celebrations that once marked the sun's long march to its June zenith.

Episcopal hymns were sung by Sir George and his men—theirs was a strict orthodox calling and their observances of its calendar were meticulous, even though they were isolated on a wild continent, an ocean away from their homes. But surely the majestic presence of the lowering December sky and the thundering curl of cold sea swells must have done more than hymns to communicate the larger presences that religion specified.

For the land, the sea, the sky, and the vast reaches of forest that span almost as much of Maine as they did then are still the primary dimensions of our Decembers. This place, even its relatively populous coast, has retained its natural integrity, and it is these natural presences that still give our Christmases a genuine center, a point of gravity that has been dissolved by time and change in many other states beyond Maine's borders.

Here in Maine, winter has arrived—a genuine winter, cold, keen, cutting, and pure, a winter whose 1607 counterpart inflicted chill and miseries on the Popham band, a winter whose definitions are never in doubt. It is thought in other places that Maine winters make Christmas a burden; life here is evidently still equated with those primitive realities of nearly four centuries back. But those who make such distant judgements do not know this state and are the lesser for it.

Yes, the cold is here, but it is more a purifier than a burden, more an exhilarator than a depressant. The ground under my boots is frost firm as I walk the dirt trail that leads into the woods, woods that reach from one end of Maine to the other, holding the state's character in place with their intertwined roots. The air is swift in my nostrils and over the feathered tops of the evergreens while white gulls glide against a gray December sky, emblems of the sea waving above a silent land. The air is softened by salt from that sea, and a few snowflakes drift like gull feathers through the trees.

If I stop and still the thumping of my boots against the hard ground, I can hear the southerly breeze in the pinetops. I can even hear the creaking of gull wings in flight. Such silence is impressive to a man who began as a city youth, who grew in a place where silence was never heard, where noise was the only constant and still is. Yet is not a kind of silence essential to understanding aspects of this season? Is it possible to share the holiday's full significance in this place that knows no peace? I think not, which is why when I stand as still as a stump in the December woods I am grateful for Maine's gift of isolation.

Thirty years have passed since my last city Christmas, and my walk in the woods is a kind of ritual observance of that departure. I come alone, trailed by thoughts of Christmas past. I can see the boy running through city streets on Christmas Eve, scouting the last of the tree sellers by their late, flickering fires, standing like trees in their overcoats pinned across sweatered chests, waiting for those they knew would come late to rescue the holiday from the shame of no Christmas evergreen.

I have remembered the paucity of those city choices and I find a kind of satisfaction in the superfluous gifts the Maine woods make. Christmas trees are spread by the thousands of square miles across most of Maine's twenty million acres, and even on the few acres I call my own a man could cut a balsam fir for every Christmas of his life and the life of his children and never hinder the forest's own renewal.

But there is enough of the city still with me to make the taking of the tree more ritual than routine. Bending there in the woods, severing the base of the trunk, I do a kind of homage to the place which has brought me such splendid abundances of solitude and Christmas trees, pure cold and exhilarating air. In my view, I am offered more treasures than I have earned, more privilege than I warrant, and yet what I have is shared by every other resident of Maine. Some, I suppose, take for granted what I am grateful for, but all of us would protest any diminution of what we have been given.

The same early darkness that compressed the brief days of Sir George and his men catches me on the way home, the tree feathering the snow as I pull it along by its butt. But our house has lighted windows, and more light spills from the door as I open it and squeeze the tree inside. Its boughs spring like a colt's legs and it showers bright droplets of melting snow across the room, a wild thing trembling at its sudden captivity. The family is there to greet me and my tree, and I know as the moment moves so splendidly around me that it is a gift from this place, this Maine.

I have made no secret of the state's generosities in the decades I have lived here. Friends and acquaintances still in the cities and suburbs often take my enthusiasms to task; they argue that I am blind to the state's realities, that I see only what I want through the tunnel vision of my romanticism. But I explain it is more their cynicism than my enthusiasms which bends their perceptions. For someone conditioned to New York's impersonal isolations, Maine's essential purity and the humanity of its people are difficult to believe. If Christmas has become a kind of commercial excess in so much of the nation, those beyond Maine argue, then there is no reason why this state should be any different. And they extend that logic (sometimes defensively I think) to apply to every other aspect of life in this most distant corner of the Northeast.

I have, from time to time, wished that every cynic, that every discouraged and jaded citizen beyond Maine's borders could somehow be brought here for a while. It would be a great gift to them to be allowed to have Christmas in Maine, to know the truth of cold, to comprehend the blessings of the solstice, to see the gulls' white banners unfurled over the evergreens, to skate on a black pond frozen silver in the moonlight, to witness the modesty of the state's Main Streets as they take the season in their stride.

No, I don't exaggerate or over embellish. Nor do I deny December. It is not an easy time. Lobstermen and fishermen (and I have been one) work with an angry and unforgiving sea. Woodsmen hew at frozen trees, and summer cottages that bloom like June flowers by lake or bay are locked and rattle in the wind, their pipes drained or shattered by frost. I have seen Christmas blizzards, Christmas sleet storms, Christmas rain, and Christmas fog. I have never told my city friends that the sun always shines here on December 25. On the contrary,

I generally assume that it will not. When it does, we mark the day
as we did one brilliant Christmas afternoon when the bay sparkled
blue and we slid the dory off the bank and took her for a row around
the point just so we could say we had been afloat on Christmas Day.

All this is a far cry from suggesting that this place, this Maine,
is a holiday Utopia where Dickens descriptions come true and the
ghosts of Christmas Past have yet to meet the often frantic spirits of
Christmas Present. Maine is certainly a part of America, and like most
American retailers, Maine's do at least a third of their year's business in
the six weeks before Christmas. And Maine's poor are not altogether
different from the city poor; I have known some lobsterman who put
codfish on their Christmas table.

But there are leveners here, lighteners of the load. To be poor
on 126th Street and Third Avenue is also to be without hope, without horizons, without relief. Maine's horizons are still unobscured;
they encourage hope instead of stifling it. And I am convinced there
is a dimension to the natural world—the woods, the water, and the
land—which is essential to the soul. No one who lives within those
dimensions can be as poor as those who are denied them by concrete
walls and fields of asphalt.

It is the gift of itself that Maine gives us at Christmas and during the entire balance of the year. But it is during these Decembers
that we yearn most for some signal that our days will not diminish
entirely, that our winters will not be endless, that our star will begin
its return. And this is why I treasure the country knowledge that the
holiday marks the start of night's retreat, that within this Christmas
week the earth, this vast entire planet, shifts its great mass and sur-
renders to the sun's insistent, incremental advance.

Few in the city are concerned with such matters as the moon's phases or the sun's advances and retreats. Air-conditioned, computerized, climate-controlled buildings without windows do not stimulate an awareness of natural rhythms. Urban and suburban Christmases have become socioeconomic events because they have been denied every natural presence. When city lights shine so brightly the stars over Manhattan cannot be seen even on a clear night, then the first Christmas symbol—and the season's astronomical anchor—is obscured. When people have no way of knowing which way the wind blows, or whence the rain comes, they fail to recognize any holiday's natural roots.

But not in Maine, and this is the genuine blessing of this place. We here mark this season as it has been marked in every northern latitude since humanity came down from the trees. Christmas extends beyond the borders of dogmas and religions to cultures the northern world around, from Maine across the Atlantic, from England across Europe and from Europe across Russia, and from Russia to the Japans beyond. It is a time when the natural and the supernatural combine; a time when we are reassured of the immortality of our sun as well as the immortality of our souls. This is the gift of Maine at Christmas.

John N. Cole wrote several books, including In Maine, *and was a frequent contributor to national magazines and newspapers such as* The New York Times *and* The Altlantic Monthly. *This essay first appeared in* Down East *magazine.*

Christmas Bells
Henry Wadsworth Longfellow
1863

I heard the bells on Christmas Day
Their old, familiar carols play,
And wild and sweet
The words repeat
Of peace on earth, good-will to men!

And thought how, as the day had come,
The belfries of all Christendom
Had rolled along
The unbroken song
Of peace on earth, good-will to men!

Till ringing, singing on its way,
The world revolved from night to day,
A voice, a chime,
A chant sublime
Of peace on earth, good-will to men!

All Is Calm

Then from the black, accursed mouth
The cannon thundered in the South,
And with the sound
The carols drowned
Of peace of earth, good-will to men!

It was as if an earthquake rent
The hearth-stones of a continent,
And made forlorn
The households born
Of peace on earth, good-will to men!

And in despair I bowed by head;
"There is no peace on earth," I said;
"For hate is strong,
And mocks the song
Of peace on earth, good-will to men!"

Then pealed the bells more loud and deep:
"God is not dead, nor doth He sleep;
The Wrong shall fail,
The Right prevail,
With peace on earth, good-will to men."

Henry Wadsworth Longfellow was born in 1807 in Portland, Maine and attended Bowdoin College beginning at age fifteen. In 1872, seven years after "I Heard The Bells on Christmas Day" was published, John Baptiste

Shannon Butler

Calkin, an English composer and organist, set the poem to music and created a Christmas song. Calkins music and Longfellow's words eventually influenced Johnny Marks who, in 1956, composed the version of "I Heard the Bells on Christmas Day" that gained widespread popularity and remains well-known today.

Christmas Day
The Oxford Democrat
1878

When Christmas morning comes, they say
The whole world knows it is Christmas Day;
The very cattle in the stalls
Kneel when the blessed midnight falls.
And all the night the heavens shines,
With luster of a light divine.
Long ere the dawn the children leap
With "Merry Christmas" in their sleep;
And dream about the Christmas tree;
Or rise, their stockings filled to see.
Swift come the hours of joy and cheer,
Of loving friend and kindred dear;
Of giving gifts and bounties in the air,
Sped by the "Merry Christmas" prayer,
While through it all, so sweet and strong,
Is heard the holy angels' song:
"Glory be to God above
On earth be peace and helpful love!

All Is Calm

And on the street, or hearts within,
The Christmas carolings begin:

Waken, Christian children
Up and let us ring
With glad voice the praises
Of our new-born King.

"Come, nor fear to seek Him,
Children though we be;
Once He said of the children,
'Let them more to me.'"

"Haste we then to welcome,
With a joyous lay,
Christ the king of glory,
Born for us to-day."

A Holiday Wish

Hallowell Weekly Register
1898

Unless the kind fates intervene, one little chap, who holds abiding faith in Santa Claus, is to be disappointed. Early in the week, he mailed a letter to Santa Claus, enumerating his Christmas wants, but unfortunately omitted his address. If anyone can give the desired address, we will try to get word to the Patron Saint of Christmas cheer. The letter read as follows:

> *Dear Mr. Santa Clause*
> *Please bring me a pair of skates. A game a polo stick and a gun picture book 1 pair overshoes legins.*

An Acadian Christmas Story

Joseph Donald Cyr

Remembering 1909

The winter of 1909 had arrived before Thanksgiving in the St. John Valley of Northern Maine. The snow reached four feet deep by Christmas Eve, despite a thaw during Advent—*le doux temps des advants.*

The village of *Lille-sur-St-Jean,* as Les Filles de la Sagesse (the Daughters of Wisdom) had called it, was in a state of high excitement. Midnight Mass was to be sung in the old church, and on New Year's Day, the first Mass would be celebrated in a new church, just completed. The year 1910 would begin with a new building, designed by a French architect living in Montreal. Many changes had been made on the interior, and the parishioners felt that it was the most beautiful church in the valley. Materials and labor had been donated and many "frolics," or work parties, had helped speed along construction and keep the cost down.

On Christmas Eve, the temperature was five below zero and the old church was decorated *en festival* for this special feast day. Four twelve-inch-wide bands of handmade lace and four bands of red satin attached to the ceiling thirty-five feet above the altar cascaded down in a graceful arc and fastened to the walls. The altar, graced by statues of *Notre Dame du Mont-Carmel* and angels, was decked in red and white flowers, the colors of the season. Candles were everywhere—electricity had not yet made its way north from Van Buren.

At nearly eleven at night and sleigh bells could be heard in every direction. Lamps on the sleighs twinkled in the moonlit night. The cold made the snow crunch loudly. Excited voices cried *"Joyeux Noël!"* The church bells pealed out and the simple, pious people were filled with emotion as they filed in under the light of kerosene lamps on the steps, laughter punctuating their small talk. Once inside, however, solemnity reigned.

Behind the old chapel the new church stood with its golden domes rising from two green and beige towers. Angels atop the domes held trumpets directed toward Canada five hundred feet away across the river—the old country, the country from which these Acadians had come for safety after their deportation from Nova Scotia in 1755.

Anastasie was excited. It was Christ's birthday. Her fourteen brothers and sisters were excited, too. Their father, Gédéon, had a special part in this historic Christmas Mass. Anastasie was six years old and this was her first midnight Mass. Her mother, Euphrosine, had prepared her. She would see Jesus in the manger tonight. The choir would sing very old Latin hymns and French carols. The air would be filled with mystery.

Whole families entered the church together and took their family pews. Candlelight filled the church and people were festive. The woodstove in the middle of the center aisle was aglow. Anastasie could feel the heat on her face as they neared it. She also could feel the blast of cold air when the door behind her opened.

Everyone scampered in quietly, genuflected, and knelt down to recite the rosary before Mass. The choir proclaimed *Les Anges dans nos Campagnes* and *Ca, Bergers, Assemblons-nous*. Mass was about to begin. Anastasie looked to the rear of the church. She could see the priest attired in white vestments with rich red and gold embroidery. The altar boys were dressed in red with white lace surplice. Anastasie looked up into the choir and saw her father in the place of honor. He started singing, "*Minuit, Chretiens!*" Its haunting melody filled the church and the congregation cried as the altar boys processed toward the altar carrying candles and the cross. The priest marched past carrying the baby Jesus to complete the manger scene.

Gédéon sang old French carols in the sleigh on the way home and the family answered him line for line. It was well after midnight as the train of sleighs followed a twisted course over the snow, you could hear other families doing the same thing. It sounded so harmonious with the church bells pealing out the joy of the season and the clatter of sleigh bells echoing across the still landscape.

The horse breathed out long streams of vapor. Stars filled the heavens and houses brimmed with excitement. The joy of Anastasie's brothers and sisters fed her own happiness. They couldn't wait to get home. Aunt Sophie had everything prepared when they arrived. Anastasie's father was the oldest in his family, so his brothers came with their families, too.

It felt warm inside and soon the house was full. All became quiet when Gédéon put the Christ child in the family crèche and prayers were spoken impatiently.

When Gédéon told the Christmas story everyone listened intently, even though they had heard it many times. Oranges and walnuts were distributed to the children—gifts from the baby Jesus. Now came the scramble for the hammer to crack the nuts. Uncle Théophile played

"*Reel du Pendu*" on the violin and was accompanied by the clatter of spoons keeping the delicate rhythms, while Thomas danced the gigue. The dancing became a competition for the best steps and Anastasie's sister, Marie-Madeline, won—at fourteen she was already a veteran of the gigue.

Anastasie saw her mother and aunts bringing out the food. Rabbit stew and ci-pâte were the mainstays. *Bûche de Noël, tarte au sucre, tarte au sirop d'érable, tarte à la mélasse, tarte aux raisins,* and *mochas* made the occasion festive.

More violin music, dancing, storytelling, and singing followed the meal, and the children were told they must go to bed.

"Christmas is so much fun. Why are Mother and Father always so glad when it's over?" Anasasie asked her oldest sister.

"You cannot understand adults until you become one," Marie-Josephe answered.

Joseph Donald Cyr is the founder and director of the Musée cultural du Mont-Carmel, which is dedicated to preserving Acadian and Québecois culture and history in the St. John Valley of Northern Maine. This piece was orginally published in Echoes *magazine.*

Christmas in Good Old Aroostook

Eva M. Furbush
1915

"Our beautiful Christmas tree is lighted with electric bulbs," said Mrs. Evans to her little daughter, Elsie. "But when I was a girl like you, I lived way down in Aroostook County, Maine, and my Christmas tree was a great green cedar about six feet tall, set up in the parlor and lighted up only by candles placed here and there, on the mantel piece, or by a large lamp on the marble center table."

"Tell me about it, mama," pleaded Elsie, looking up earnestly into her eyes. Picture books were forgotten, blocks were uninteresting; and dolls took a back seat when mother started to tell about her girlhood. It had been a long and beautiful day for Elsie, and as her bedtime was creeping near, mother thought it was a good opportunity to tell her a story, no matter the subject, so that tired little eyes might gradually close, and tired little hands lay still in peaceful slumber.

"It was like this, Elsie," mother began, "we were a large family of brothers and sisters; one big tree held all our family gifts, so there was not really much room left for the electric bulbs, even if we had owned any of such luxuries in those early days. Then, too, the shadows in our great parlor played all around our tree, the flickering candles throwing such waxy gleams over all our treasured gifts and homemade decorations that it was real mysterious and Christmasy to sit in the stiff-backed horsehair parlor chairs, and watch the little shiny ornaments flitter now and then and see the long strings of popcorn gleam all snowy-white against the dark green of the boughs. We had wonderful bags of candy showing through the meshes; we had candy canes, gingerbread dolls; fancy worked mottoes; rolls of print; books, new shoes, mufflers knit by mother's busy hands; shawls, caps, skates, dolls—but the dolls were not much like yours, dearie."

"How did the dolls look, mother?" asked Elsie

"Well, I remember one doll I had that was adorned with white lace-trimmed underwear and her dress was of dark blue wool goods, also her bonnet, and her face was charmingly hand painted by a clever dressmaker who had fashioned her clothes. I think my aunt Sophia paid exactly two dollars for the doll, and to my mind she was just about as fine as could be."

"Would she say 'mamma' and 'papa' when you squeezed her?"

"No," laughed mother, "she was not at all up-to-date like your dollies. Our Christmas day in Maine was not complete without a good snowball fight, a ride on our sleds, or a sleighride, if the snow was not too deep. Oh, how the old bells used to jingle! Automobiles are pretty fine, but they have not yet invented one that will produce a thrill like the good old sleigh of olden days. When they get one that will slide along over the crusty snow with a jingle of merry bells, why then they will have invented something worthwhile."

"Did you like the snow, mamma?"

"Oh, yes, I loved it; we would make snow ice cream sometimes; put some clean white snow in a bowl, add several spoonfuls of sugar, a few drops of flavoring, and turn some sweet milk over the snow, then eat it with our spoons. "Sugaring off" was another delicious time for us youngsters in the spring. Making snowmen and forts out in the barn yard, shoveling wide paths to the barn and clothes yard, going to school after the Christmas holidays and telling of all the new gifts received was only part of the glorious days of my childhood. You little folks, nowadays, have no idea how much fun it was to play, and now have everything bought for you out of a model department store, with a "Made in Germany" stamped on the back of it.

A lot of us young folks would get a pung and ride to the grange hall for a singing social, and each would bring a box of goodies to be opened and feast. The boys and girls would dance for hours and the old folks would sit and watch and gossip harmless news.

Sometimes my sister would play the old melodeon on Christmas Eve and the whole family would gather 'round her and sing heartily those dear old tunes, "God Rest Ye Merry Gentlemen," "There Is No Place Like Home," "Bluebells of Scotland," and others. There was a lullaby that my mother used to sing:

"As I wandered round the homestead
Every dear familiar spot,
Seemed to bring recollection,
Thing I'd seemingly forgot.
There the orchard meadow yonder,
Here the deep old-fashioned well,
With its old moss-covered bucket,
Sent a thrill no tongue can tell."

Mrs. Evans bent and kissed the curly head lying on her shoulder, so deep in slumber that the last strains of the lullaby fell on silent ears.

Christmas on the Lightship
Hal Cram
1925

The spirit of Christmas is in the air. You will find it everywhere. In the homes of the rich and the poor, in the cities and in the country, even on the palatial liners as they ply through the seas to and from Europe, and on the fishing vessels that happen to be obliged to spend the holidays on the banks. You will find it, too, in the lighthouses among the men who aid in guiding the toilers of the sea into a snug harbor. You will find it on our lightships, tossing about in foam-covered seas.

Anchored in places too difficult to build a lighthouse, lightships guide vessels safely into harbors with the lights on their masts. Ten miles from Portland Harbor and seven and three quarters miles south southeast of Portland Head Light, the lightship Portland No. 76 tugs at its mooring. Built in Virginia twenty-three years ago, the craft has been moored on its present station, with few exceptions, practically ever since its launching. Within its hull, many holidays have been observed by the officers and crew, and many exciting and thrilling incidents have been witnessed from its solid decks. Just now, the population of this little floating village numbering twelve people are making their plans for the Yuletide holiday.

Down in the ship, where it is as warm and comfortable as any home on land, there will be the Christmas tree attractively decorated with its usual colored trinkets and lights, while here and there on the green boughs will be the presents each man makes to the others, presents, too, that the relief boat will bring to the ship this month, presents from the families of the men, which will bear the usual words, "Not to be opened until Christmas." The dinner table will be graced in its center with one of the largest and finest turkeys obtainable, and there will be all the Christmas fixings; the candies and cakes, the jokes and the surprises, for what is man, anyway, but overgrown boy.

The men enjoy a nine-day shore leave every month, or 108 days each year; consequently there will be some among the crew who will be able to eat their Christmas dinner with their families at their homes. But those who are left behind on the lightship are not downhearted for they will make merry, and their Uncle Sam will see to it that they are enjoying to the utmost the spirit of the day.

It is, therefore, up to the elements to come forth with good weather, and allow the officers and the crew as much relaxation as possible. A heavy storm with thick weather keeps everyone aboard the craft busy, each having their respective duties to perform. Holidays cannot interfere with duty, and this is especially true on board a lightship. The fog horn must be kept blowing, the lights in operation, and the submarine bell striking the ship's number at regular intervals.

It is the southeast storm that the men on the lightship dread the worst. The seas are mountain high, and time and again break over the craft, making it almost impossible for anyone to be on deck. There are many times when the waist of the lightship is filled to the brim with foaming green water, when the craft trembles with every tug on the 150-fathom chain attached to a six-thousand-pound mushroom anchor. It is such times when the waves are crashing against the sides of the ship, when the low drab scudding clouds seem to pass through the very top masts, that everything depends upon the strength of every link in the big chain, for as the saying goes, "A chain is but as strong as its weakest link." Should the chain part during a heavy gale from the southeast, it would only be a comparatively short time before the craft would pile up on the numerous ledges which are not far distant from the ship's mooring ground.

A wind from the northeast, or northwest, or in fact most any other wind except southeast, no matter how hard it blows, barely brings a wrinkle to the man on the Portland No. 76. At such times, if the chain parted, the ship would simply be blown to sea, and, as it is so constructed that it would keep afloat in almost anything, even a hurricane, there would be the chance that the craft could make its way back to the anchorage or to shelter under its own steam.

The officers aboard the lightship are Captain George K. Martin of Lubec, Chief Engineer Eldridge G. Pinkham of Portland, and Assistant Engineer Charles E. Butler of Franklin. The mate is Asbury Hanna of Round Pond. These men are appointed from Washington. The cook, two firemen, and five sailors are hired by the Captain. There is always someone on watch, beginning with the mate from six to eight each evening. From eight until five o'clock in the morning the watch is divided among the five sailors, each doing a turn of something like two hours. The cook then comes on for the hour between five and six, and keeps watch while he prepares breakfast.

If it is day, just as soon as the mainland at Portland Head Light is shut from view by either fog, rain, or mist, or snow or vapor in the winter, the fog whistle and submarine bell are started. At night, the light is turned on just as soon as darkness obscures the shoreline.

In thick or stormy weather nearly all the crew are on duty, and work like yeoman to guard the lives of those who may happen to be on the deep. The submarine bell when lowered into the water remains about thirty feet under the surface. At that point it is operated by twin hose receiving compressed air from the engine room. It is all automatic, the wheel causing the bell to strike having seven cams, then a short space followed by six cams. This allows the bell to strike the number of the ship. Pilots of steamers coming into Portland have spoken of the lightship, stating that they have heard the submarine bell as far away as twenty miles, a much greater distance than the surface bell buoy can be heard. It is also estimated that the sound of the bell is transmitted under the water at a speed one-third faster than is possible through the air.

The lightship is anchored in about thirty fathom of water and is there for the purpose of providing pilots of steamers or vessels with a mark, whereby they can by night or in thick weather sail on a direct course from that point into Portland Harbor, passing all ledges and reefs without danger. It might be added that there are plenty of rocks between the lightship and Portland Head Light, and before the days of Portland No. 76, many craft came to an untimely end.

One of the officers of the lightship informed me that only once in the last eighteen years has the ship dragged its anchor, and then only for a distance of about a mile. This happened during an extra heavy Norther, but as the craft dragged in a direction where there was no danger of being wrecked, there was little fear aboard ship, and within forty-eight hours, the boat was back on its mooring. The only other times that it has been off its stationing during the past eighteen years was when it was called to do duty for a time during the war when she was anchored off Staten Island, New York, and also for a time off

Portsmouth. Every two years, the boat comes to the dry dock in Portland for examination, repairs, painting, and scraping.

We 'uns of Portland and Maine, wish you 'uns of the Portland Lightship a very Merry Christmas and a Happy New Year, and may the holidays be hours when the sea remains calm, when Kris Kringle can tie his reindeer to your topmasts and slide down into the forecastle for a general good time.

A lightship was a ship that acted as a lighthouse in areas where lighthouses couldn't be built. They were moored in places deemed dangerous for passing ships and were equipped with lights and sounds to warn approaching sailors of hazards. The lightship Portland No. 76 was stationed in Portland Harbor, five miles southeast of Cape Elizabeth, and was in use from 1903 to 1933.

Visiting a Lumber Camp for Christmas
Lucina H. Lombard
1929

When I left Portland, the morning after a day's heavy rain, the streams were open and the sun shining warm, something unusual in mid-December. At Bath, that noon, the channel had to be cut ahead of the boat. It was snowing hard and blowing worse when we crossed Frenchman's Bay— "the roughest part of the Maine coast in a squall," the Captain told us. In Bangor, it was cold and windy with nice hard snowy streets. We tumbled into bed at midnight with a six o'clock call for breakfast—which by the way, we did not have time for—just drunk some excellent coffee provided by the well-known hotel. Then we took the Bangor and Aroostook to Monticello (where there was four feet of snow on a level), for a winter's teaching, and incidentally, a series of odd, yet pleasant experiences, which often made us feel that we were in a dream, a bit backwoodsy and crude but altogether *kindly.*

From the first, "we were shown" a lot, not because we were from Missouri, but from "outside." The older generations call us "Kinne-beckers," although, in vain, we insisted that we lived on the banks of the Saco.

One of our first Saturdays outings, courteously planned for our entertainment, was a trip to a lumber camp. Every winter, usually near Christmas time, this was the custom. "Many of them are towns-boys and men," we were told, "with a mixture of French-Canadian wood-choppers and a sprinkling of queer ones who furnish the fun."

It was an Arctic Saturday dropped down into our variegated New England year. The sun beamed red in the morning sky, and the keen hoar frost crisps to our hurrying feet as we climb into the pung drawn by a couple of beautiful Dack horses—Canadian beauties.

On the first lap of our fourteen-mile drive, we realized that we needed the fur coat that a friend had thoughtfully provided. There were a dozen people in our party. We breathe deep with a sense of abounding life as glad and free and unrestricted as that of the birds or the northwest wind. A sky of intense blue arches above out heads, infinitely removed from our "too, too solid earth," where today neutral tints rule.

This northern projection of our state thrusts far up between New Brunswick and Southern Quebec. Monticello is a border town, in the first range of townships bordering on New Brunswick. This location was of importance in its early settlement, as supplies could come in via the St. John River, from Woodstock, only twelve miles distant. We are only three miles from the river on the old Military Road— a legacy of the Aroostook War—put through when the boundary dispute was in its acute state, and becoming the great thoroughfare over which immigration flowed into this northern country. Civilization has followed almost exactly the print of the moccasin. On the old trail this side of the St. John are still Indian camps which furnish our snowshoes. Ahead of us and to our right is Mars Hill, 1,800 feet high, the mountain which British surveyors, in 1826, claimed to be the highlands referred to in the treaty of 1783. The American survey-ors dissented, and these two claims formed one of the causes of that bloodless war. The mountain stands just inside the boundary line as now established and is the lone sentry of the "New Northeast."

Dome-shaped hills and ridges with valleys between extended along the north branch of the Meduxnekeag, a tributary of the St. John, and itself in turn supplied from several lakes.

Starch factories take care of the small potatoes, the overflow from the potato houses seen on every large farm. Flocks of sheep sun themselves in runs beside the barns. We moved past broad fields of this "Garden of Maine," where wheat, oats, barley, and buckwheat are raised, the latter the staples which (together with its spruce) causes this section to be called The Land of Spruce Gum and Buckwheat Cakes.

The soil peculiar to Eastern Aroostook is a rich vegetable loam from two to five feet thick (with no rocks, not even gravel). This is underlain by the calcareous slate and crumbly limestone formation, which is continually working up to the surface. This causes the farmers' toil to yield the hundred-fold promised in Scripture.

In the snowy fields around us, the snow has drifted over the four-feet high cedar rail fences (built seventy years before); and we see groves of beech and maple on the slopes, the black of the tamarack, and the yellow of cedar along streams, and moose bogs! We pass a wild spot, whence you may gaze down the huge trough of a cedar-fringed, slaty-ledged gorge into a valley. All around is a wilderness scarcely broken. Nearby is "Desolation Siding" its tamaracks replacing the ancient glory of the pines. We see a line of cars loaded with potatoes, grain, and lumber; the tawny flare of locomotives' fires the heavy rumble of wheels one listens to is one of the pulse-beats of the nation.

A haunt for birds: Trains drop stray grain along, which, if not eaten then, springs up to make more food later on.

Now, we turn into the wood-road leading to Plantation No. 13. There are 23,040 acres in this six-mile square piece of forested land, which is only one of our 450 of these tracts of land, totaling 9,000,000 acres in Maine: a grand square of approximately 120 miles on each side, so that it is 480 miles around this square, and one side of it is about equal to the distance from Portland to Boston. Such is the magnitude of the area of "the wild lands of Maine, her greatest single property—richer than Nevada's golden peaks."

The dense forest wilderness into which we have plunged we traverse with little intermission for nearly ten miles. There was a thrill for the "outsider" in the spectacle—in the untried mystery of the forest, miles beneath the over-hanging branches of encircling trees.

On snow scenes tinted with purple shadows and the green of the spruce we feasted our eyes. We heard of "potato lords" and "timber barons," and now Holman Day's books began to be illuminated with understanding.

The streams are brooks up where the timber stands. We came to such a one now, ice-bound, with its beaver dam, and sharply outlined against a background of towering pines, the camp with its cheerful line of ascending smoke.

"They are always glad to have come," said one of the girls.

We were greeted by the camp cook, a big, blue-eyed cordial fellow, whose sole purpose just now seemed to be the comfort of our party.

The warmth of the fire streamed through the open door. Inside, we found that a long table, shelves, benches, and couches made a comfortable dining room with the kitchen at the other end of the long room of the log cabin.

"We shall find wholesome fare here," said one of the men, whose chief concern was always "something to eat."

In a few minutes we were warm and rested and ready for dinner. The woodsmen had already eaten their noon meal and gone back to work. The bare board tables were scrubbed clean, and upon them were arranged plates, dippers, and spoons of tin, supplemented by steel knives and forks.

We had baked beans, pickles, bread and butter, doughnuts, and coffee, all of them excellent. The men went out to where the woodsmen were at work. We were now ready for exploration. The "wise heads" of the party had decided which side trail to take. It was one of those still winter days when even the wind seems bound by the hard frost. The sliding snow-shoes creaked shrilly. The swamped out path winds up a slight ascent, through wide-spreading spruces into stately white pines and swaying hemlocks with here and there a towering Norway (red) pine. Then down the southern slope where chickadees are calling in the sunny opening, we fight our way through tangles of underbrush, scrambling around steep places, slipping, holding on by tree trunks for the snow is slippery from last week's ice storm, down, down, down—and finally into the hollow of the brook; then gradually up again to the straggle of trees on a hard wood ridge, with tangled undergrowth of moose-wood (striped maple) whose pliant wands the moose and deer love to nibble, witch hobble, and mountain jolly.

Holman Day in his *King Spruce* says, "Old winter himself had pitched camp there and mixed up a batch of the right kind of weather. With much deliberation, he patted down the fluff under the big trees with beating sleety rains, and when the ground was ready for the sowing of the mighty crop, he piled his banks of clouds up from the south, and though he gave the coast folks rain, he brought the men of the north woods what they were longing for—snow a plenty; snow that heaped the arms of the spruces, filled the air with smooth clouds and blanketed the ground."

The tapering firs in the dark places, where snow still bent down their branches, were the most beautiful sight of all. These bushed sanctuaries of fir, wrapped like the Holy Grail, in napkins of snowy linen let fall from heaven—can they be a part of the prosaic "outside" world of the hurrying city?

As we go on, there are raftered Viking halls festooned with snow for the Winter Feast. Here are century old trees—a sacred grove if ever was one worthy to be a place of worship. Winter rigor is seal and symbol of our northern races. We need it for the good of our souls.

The forest here is peculiary rich with layers and layers of green boughs, as though they had been heaped there especially for the winter holiday. *Swish, swish,* came a peculiar sound. But it was but a wandering breeze in the low spruces.

Our snowshoes searched out the path unconsciously as it wound this way and that. Low growing scrub caught at them making progress difficult, so we returned back, reaching camp at sunset.

Several birds new to us, but which the cookee told us were Moosebirds, were picking scraps which he had just thrown out. "The Indians call him Wiscashion," he added. It was the gray day which calls socially, "What cheer, what cheer?" to hunters and lumbermen.

The fire in the huge stove was welcome after the frosty air. While the lumberman ate, we stayed in "the office," an alcove partially curtained off from the dining room, for the use of the bookkeeper and boss.

Then we feasted on warm ginger cookies and what we afterward learned was bear steak. One could never have told it from beef!

The boss had rapped an enormous pine to see if it was hollow (such oversize trees usually are) when they were surprised to hear a growling. Mistrusting it was a bear's winter home, he sent a man for his gun. The bear was soon dispatched, and a generous supply of meat procured. The two cubs were sent down to Houlton to be sold.

We dreaded a bit the ordeal of entering the other camp where the men's living room was where they lounged away on the "deacon seat" their precious three hours of rest between supper and bedtime.

Besides the Yankees, there were several types of Canadians, each standing as a page of the country's history, summing up the early days of Canada, when endurance and courage of no ordinary stamp were required to meet the want, the wars, and the hardships of their struggle.

From November until April, most of these men were shut in by the bleak winter's work with few or no chances to visit their homes. Little wonder they hailed our coming as a welcome break in monotony. For neither books, magazines nor an occasional paper (if they can read) can take the place of the homes they have left, be they ever so humble, nor the home folks there, but they accustom themselves to these details of life.

Yet, for each, there is the capacity to dream dreams, that elusive something that gold cannot buy when Christmas is near. The magic of folklore, the stories told by the grandparents when they were children, now pieced together bit by bit, figuring in the patchwork of forgotten memory. The tales had been half-forgotten; but here they come back like Kate Nickleby's miniature, "unmoved, unchanged," this being the quality of all good miniatures and of really good stories.

Several are making odd little toys: playthings for the youngsters at home. One young chap is carving a wooden fan, a pretty keepsake for his best girl.

"Mac" was regaling those with an ear for music by cheerful efforts on his mouth harp, jigging the heel of his moccasined foot for time.

Another was whistling dolefully, but the tune was about a "red, red robin."

Our men had brought candy, nuts, and oranges for the crowd. The woodsmen gave us their store of fragrant spruce gum.

Someone asks Pete to sing one of his Canuck songs. After that 'tis easy. Song follow song. "Jack," who teaches the "backwoods" school, is a Boston University graduate and does his bit, a humorous skit, which all forty of the lumbermen vigorously applaud.

One of the "born storytellers" gives his version of a moose hunt he and his chum shared just before he came into camp. Another fellow with a story of being chased by a "Devil"—the big Canadian lynx that goes drifting through the forest on soundless feet, feet that on the merest provocation can be turned into deadly flesh-tearing weapons of destruction. We shiver at the tale of the great tawny cat more dreaded than any other creature of the Maine woods now that wolves have left Maine.

An Englishman says that during the Yule season, especially during the three days after Christmas, it was thought to be risky to go abroad, for then the spirits of dead warriors raced with the gods about the world on the wind; Odin, the wild huntsman, with fire-breathing dogs, snaring souls and putting them in his huntsman's pouch driving the moon-eyed Futursel, a white owl, before him. Thor also, in his cart drawn by goats, whirling his hammer and with his red beard streaming auroral lights athwart the sky. Freyr riding on a boar. There were other goddesses also, hunting with their hounds through the clouds.

That little patch of light in the cabin with the black brooding forest around, was a fit setting for these wild stories. The blue smoke from pipe bowls and cigarettes curls up to mingle with the shadows of the bracket lamps against the low ceiling. The dominant power of good will is the test of life; not the tangible, visible things that people give at Christmas. So that spirit was present with us.

The timekeeper began playing on a harmonica, "God Rest You, Merry Gentlemen." As we sang the old carol, one would say there could be no glamour here, there is such a light in all the hearts, that their souls—if never at other times—wake in the Christmas season from their long sleep.

Good-nights are said, and we go out into the clear, cold, night air in the depths of the forest. The crisp snow creaked under the runners and the bells sang fairy tunes in time with the feet of the hurrying horses. The owls, who awake at sundown, hooted at us, as the road wound on under the trees.

Out of the shadows of the woods into the shimmer of starlight with the moon holding her lantern for us. The moon light is creeping down the hill slopes, while all the northland seems beaming with splendid light—the "Northern Lights"—which man never cease to wonder over.

And so home—and so to bed.

Wishing for a Merry Christmas

Thomas Hanna

Remembering 1932

With Roosevelt's election victory behind us, and my father's door-to-door sales supplementing his caretaker's income, I had high hopes that the Christmas of 1932 in Georgetown would be merrier than the last. Ever since I could remember, my father had warned us that Santa Claus didn't have many toys to give out in such hard times, but I had my doubts about Santa. He usually left a lot of toys—and much better ones—at my friends' houses, making me think that he had left some of our toys elsewhere by mistake. I figured my mother ought to write Santa a letter and get it straightened out. I was still hoping to get a tricycle from him, although there was always a chance I'd find it under the church Christmas tree instead.

Every fall along about November, my Grandpa Rowe wrote letters to the summer people and asked them to donate money for a Christmas Fund, which he used to buy presents for all the needy children in Five Islands. I didn't believe there was anyone in town more in need of a trike than I, and I couldn't think of anyone more deserving. Didn't I have the Sunday School attendance stars to show for it, and a consecration certificate to boot? And didn't I know by heart the story of how seventy-five years ago, the people in the village had taken apart the old church at Robinhood, brought it to Five Islands piece by piece, and built this beautiful building next to the cemetery?

With Grandpa Rowe buying all those church gifts, I didn't think a little hint from me would do any harm. During those early days I knew him a lot better than I knew Grampa Hanna. I saw a lot more of him. He was the Five Islands postmaster, and the post office was inside Savage's store. When he wasn't doing postal business, he worked out front with Percy. Sometimes, when Percy was attending to his plumbing business, Grandpa Rowe ordered supplies and stocked Percy's shelves for him. I can still see him standing behind the counter, wrapped in his gray grocer's smock, a ruddy-faced man with prematurely white hair. A stale cigar butt dangled full-time from the corner of his mouth and waggled whenever he talked.

Born in 1880, he was close to twenty years younger than my Grampa Hanna, and his outgoing manner stood in sharp contrast to Grampa Hanna's quiet ways. He enjoyed a good joke, and when he told one he laughed just as hard as when we told ours. In addition to my mother, Grandpa Rowe had another daughter, Helen, with his second wife, Geneva, who had raised my mother. Helen was thirteen years younger than my mother. Grandpa was a good sort, even though many in town avoided him when they'd see him coming. Many of the poor Five Islanders owed money on their accounts at the store, and they didn't want to face him.

Grandpa Rowe made regular Sunday visits to the bungalow while Geneva took supper with her sister. He never stayed for a meal; he just came to see his grandchildren.

Christmas was drawing nigh and my trike prospects were still dim. I figured it was time to bend Grandpa's ear about that three-wheeler. One Sunday afternoon I waited for him to show up. Like always, he took the shortcut through the woods, past Hite's Pond, over the neighbor's stone wall, and across the ledges to our front door (which was still in the back).

He was barely seated on the divan when I climbed into his lap and took his gold watch from his vest pocket. When he asked me what time it was, I piped right up and told him it was almost time for Santa to come and bring me my trike, which I had a great need for. My mother had already told him I had an even greater need for warm clothes, but all he said to me was that a trike was a pretty tall order. Then he changed the subject, like he wanted to take my mind off Christmas. "Knock, knock," he said.

"Who's there?" I came right back.

"Sadie."

"Sadie who?"

"Just Sadie word and I'll be there."

I hit him with one of my own. "Knock, knock, Grandpa."

"Who's there?"

"Chester."

"Chester who?"

"Chester song at twilight."

We all shared a hearty laugh, as though either of the jokes rated it. Grandpa was just hitting his stride. "Got a riddle for you, Tommy. Now pay close attention. A man went to a prison to visit a prisoner. When someone asked who the prisoner was, he replied, 'Brothers and sisters have I none, but that man's father is my father's son.' Who was the prisoner?"

I struggled so hard with that one for the rest of his visit that I forgot to mention the Christmas trike again before he left. Grandpa wouldn't tell me the answer. I'd have to figure it out for myself, he said. He never did tell me, and by the time I finally figured out that the man was visiting his son, I don't recall whether I bothered to tell him I'd gotten it.

In late November, my hopes for a decent Christmas brightened. A package the size of an orange crate came in the mail from the Boynton family. Christmas presents, I was told. When I wondered out loud why the Boyntons had our Christmas presents, my father explained that sometimes Santa gave our gifts to them to send to us. I thought it strange Santa would leave our presents with Summer Complaints, but I didn't really care how they came as long as they arrived by Christmas. The Boyntons collected used toys, clothing, and books from the other Malden Island families and sent them to the Hannas. My mother put the box away until later. "This is not for prying eyes," she warned. "And I don't want to catch anyone peeking."

The arrival of the gifts seemed to fill my mother with the Christmas spirit. She said it was high time I spoke a piece at the Christmas concert. The director gave me a short poem about Baby Jesus in the manger and I was supposed to memorize it before Christmas. My mother worked with me every evening until I had it down pat.

As the holiday eve approached, Cora, Irving, and I took to standing by the chimney and hollering up at Santa. He never really said much to us on those occasions. He usually let us know he was up there, though. He'd make a funny little "Ho-ho" noise in a voice that sounded a lot like my mother's.

A week before Christmas, my father took me into the woods. We picked out a Christmas tree and he set it up in the living room. My mother broke out the box of colored balls and the few pieces of tinsel and garland she had brought with her from her childhood home. Cora, Irving, and I sat at the kitchen table cutting up strips of paper, coloring them with red and green crayons, and pasting them together to make a chain that we draped over the tree. It was a beautiful tree. I loved the cheery twinkle of the balls as they caught the flickering lamplight.

On the afternoon of Christmas Eve, my mother scrubbed our necks and ears, combed our hair, and shined our shoes. We ate an early supper and, just after dark, we piled into the Model A for the short haul to church. Just before we left, I went to the chimney corner and called up, "Hey Santa Claus, are you up there?"

As usual, all he said was, "Ho-ho."

This time, I persisted. "Santa, I need a trike."

Santa again said, "Ho-ho."

My father took my arm and scooted me out the door.

The church was brightly lit with kerosene lamps in sconces on the walls and a goodly crowd was filing in. Christmas Eve brought out many new faces. Some were parents whose children usually came without them, but they came now to hear their little ones speak their pieces. They'd be back again come Easter Sunday. We children were herded down to the front near the stage beneath the pulpit. To our right, in the corner, stood the tree, a tall spruce that scraped the ceiling.

I couldn't keep my eyes off it. Among its tinseled branches, I could see dozens of packets in Christmas wrappings. On the floor around the base were more. I didn't see a tricycle.

I fidgeted in my seat until the concert got under way. After some praying and carol singing, we kids said our pieces. When it came my turn, I dashed up onto the stage to the exact spot the director had marked, looked out into the crowd and spoke in my loudest voice:

Long ago in Bethlehem,
In a manger filled with hay,
The baby Jesus Christ was born.

I started to leave the stage, but the director motioned me back and held up one finger. There was one more line. I hurried back to the spot.

On that first Christmas day.

Then I dashed back to my seat while the grown-ups chuckled and my parents beamed. Nobody clapped; it wasn't permitted in the house of the Lord.

After the final prayers, Grandpa handed out the presents. There was no tricycle for me, only socks, a union suit, and a sweater. Cora got a Flying Arrow sled. Disappointed, I tucked my presents under my arm, climbed into the Model A and rode home.

My mother got us undressed and ready for bed. She said I could sleep in my new union suit. I'd need it, she said, because tonight would be one of those below-zero nights. She spread our coats over our blankets for good measure. After the "Now I lay me down to sleep" prayers, I stood by the chimney and made one last plea to Santa. This time, he didn't even answer. I crawled back into bed, pulled my coat over my head, and fell asleep thinking about that trike.

On Christmas morning, we children awoke before dawn. The house was frigid, the stoves full of yesterday's ashes. I gave my father his Christmas wake-up call. "Can we get up now?" I sang out from under the covers.

"Not until I build the fires," came the reply.

There was nothing to do but wait until he rolled out. I got up to use the chamber mug. The floor was like ice and I was glad I'd slept with my socks on. I peeked through the curtain that hung in the doorway between our bedroom and the living room, but in the darkness I couldn't see anything. "It's no fair peeking," my mother had said, so I climbed back under the covers and listened as my father shook down the grates in the kitchen, then lit a lamp in the living room and built a roaring fire in the potbellied stove. Around the edge of the curtain I could barely see a limb of the tree. I turned my head away. I wouldn't peek.

"You can come out now," my father yelled. I was the first one out. Right away I spotted the tricycle. The tag attached to the handlebars said FOR TOMMY. I recognized that trike. It had belonged to one of my cousins and I'd ridden it at his house. Did I care? No; it was every bit as good as new to me.

I ignored the rest of the gifts under the tree and hopped onto the trike. My father lifted me off it and set it aside. "You can play with that later, after we've seen all the presents."

He sat us down and handed out our presents one by one. He reached far under the tree, came out with a toy steam shovel and handed it to me. It had a long crane with a bucket on the end. You could lower it to pick up a load of dirt and then crank it back up. It would be just the thing to load dirt into Irving's new dump truck when we built more roads behind the house. I noticed that the bright yellow paint was chipped in a few places. We'd have to write and tell Santa to be a little more careful with my toys in the future.

There were other gifts for all of us and a stocking for each of us hung by the chimney. I was too busy with my shovel and tricycle to notice what anyone else got, and as soon as everything had been opened, I climbed back onto my trike.

"Keep that thing out of the kitchen," my father warned. "Your mother will be cooking Christmas dinner." He had gotten a small chicken and my mother was peeling squash and potatoes. This was turning out to be a fine Christmas.

We all sat down to a roast chicken dinner with all the fixings. My father had brought his appetite to the table and managed to eat a little of everything, except the stuffing. Afterward, he stayed out of the baking soda and remarked to my mother that his ulcer must be getting better; he should be ready for Malden Island come spring.

By bedtime, when I put away my trike, I guessed this had been about the best Christmas anyone could have.

Thomas Hanna was a longtime resident of Bath, Maine, but grew up in the Midcoast village of Five Islands or Georgetown, Island. This essay originally appeared in his memoir, Shoutin' into the Fog.

Christmas in a One-Room School
May B. Davidson
Remembering 1934

My school days began in a one-room school in Bremen. The year was 1934. One teacher, Miss Fossett of Round Pond, taught all subjects to eight grades and somehow provided us with a solid, basic education. She covered all capacities from general cleaning, filling, and polishing oil wall lamps, keeping the wood stove going, and being second mother to fifteen or twenty scholars, as we were called then. The number of scholars fluctuated over time and there were only twelve during my years there.

Our "school bus" was an old, tired, wood-sided "Beech Wagon." It's Isinglass windows had long since cracked and blown away. We were kept from freezing in winter by a huge, thickly-furred buffalo hide over our knees.

The school did not have a well, so two older boys were required to bring pails of water from a neighbor's house, about a quarter mile up the road. Gaiety along the way sometimes resulted in limited water arriving to fill the barrel-shaped crock with a small spigot at the bottom. The boys also brought in big chunks of wood from the entryway to pile around the stove.

All Is Calm

We created our own drinking cups by folding paper into the proper shape, but it was usually flimsy "arithmetic" paper that went soggy and leaked before we finished drinking. We were happy on days when there was only blue-lined writing paper available to make cups because it held water longer, giving us more time to waste. Also, the blue lines had a fascinating way of dissolving and running down the inside of the cup staining the water with veils of color.

When morning chores were done we were seated. Our day began by saluting the flag, reciting the Lord's Prayer, and singing a hymn. Handwritten papers, which Miss Fossett had prepared the evening before, and daily assignments for each grade were passed out.

As the morning wore on and the loud tick-tock of the wooden octagonal wall clock with its roman numerals and shining pendulum seemed to be slowing down for us, the teacher's announcement— "You may lay your work aside for recess"—reenergized us and filled us with new life for the mid-morning and mid-afternoon. Noon hours seemed wonderfully long and after the "dinner pail" contents were devoured, we built snow forts, had snowball battles, or went skating on nearby Webber Lake.

When we returned to the afternoon's lessons we were deeply encrusted with snow, and little pills of ice rattled on our mittens. All removable clothing was spread on the wood stacked by the stove. The wettest of us were allowed to pull our desks into a circle around it. I can still smell the steaming wool of our hats and mittens.

To begin our afternoon session, Miss Fossett read aloud two chapters of an adventure story; this was the highlight of our day. Our energy had been used playing in the snow, and our interest in studies waned. There were two diversions: A bitterly cold visit to the outhouse or the pleasure of watching the banner rats at play.

These engaging creatures are not rats, but large and pretty mice, round-eared, soft-eyed, nearly blonde and sport fluffy banners at their tail ends. The mice lived in the entry's wood pile, and had chewed small arches in the baseboard between entry and school room. They came out to watch us, sitting up and grooming their white tummies. We learned to enjoy them silently because Miss Fossett viewed them as wretched rodents and went after them with a broom if she divined the direction of our gaze.

Another break we favored was when the Ipana Toothpaste salesman came to visit the school and distributed small samples of the yellow tubes with red stripes that converged in the center. When his lecture about dental health was finished, and he left, we squeezed the toothpaste out and ate it with gusto since candy was not affordable in this era of 1930s. It was vaguely sweet and minty.

From November on we looked forward eagerly to Christmas at school. We were in the Great Depression years, and Christmas was simple, if not stark, for all of us, but it did not affect our joy and anticipation of Christmas activities.

As the time neared, first in the celebration was the expedition for a Christmas tree. I particularly remember the Christmas when I was nine years old. On the day chosen to cut the tree, one of the eighth grade boys brought an ax to school, and then our teacher lead all twelve scholars off into the woods. There were miles of pine, spruce, and balsam forest growing just across the road from our school. Thirsting for adventure we tramped along with Miss Fossett, laughing, throwing snowballs, and searching for the perfect balsam tree. Sometimes we stooped to caress the moss on a ledge, or found some frozen red wintergreen berries, so piquantly flavorful.

Once we were deeply into the woods and were standing quietly still for a short rest, a magnificent bull moose crossed ahead of us. Ignoring us, we watched his sleek, dark body silently disappear, his head bent back to maneuver his great antlers through the branches. His noble beauty was breathtaking.

When we found a classic balsam fir, it was cut and the boys shouldered it back to school. To decorate it, we cut and glued colorful paper chains and popped popcorn so we could string it on the tree. We also brought out carefully stored ornaments to hang on the branches. A kind retired doctor who lived nearby provided a practical gift for each child to be placed under the tree, which stood from floor to ceiling filling the room with its pungent fragrance, the essence of Christmas.

Later in the season, Miss Fossett gave us each a piece to learn and recite, and guided the older children in the production of a Christmas play. With practice we performed it quite well, until, that is, our parents came to school to join our Christmas celebration. As they watched, stage fright took over, and we mumbled our lines or delivered them in rapid-fire staccato lest our memory should fail before we finished.

The youngest scholar was little five-year-old Annie in the first grade. She was the last in a family of lusty older brothers. Annie had a lisp and she was squirming nervously in her first public appearance. As she struggled with her lisping recitation she suddenly burst out, "Thit! Mumma! My panth ith fallin' down!"

Annie's mother went to the rescue, and Miss Fossett hurried to the ancient organ to pump out a Christmas carol hoping to distract from the scene. She succeeded because it was another amusing event. The music was jarringly discordant because the banner rats nest in the organ and chewed some of the vital notes that were in their way. The entertainment ended joyfully. Each child's gift of a book and mittens from under the tree was excitedly opened, and apple cider, with homemade doughnuts provided by Miss Fossett were passed around.

Thinking back to the simplicity and innocence of Christmas at the one-room school in Bremen still brings pangs of nostalgia each year as I remember the drenching scent of balsam, the warmth of the woodstove, the softness of kerosene lamplight. A beautiful time that has passed. I think of school children who may have never experienced the joy of following their teacher into the holiness of an old and deep evergreen forest, never listened to the silken silence of it, never seen a huge wild animal in his own forest setting, or bent to touch velvet mosses while searching for the perfect Christmas tree.

Yes, in those early times larger, city schools may have offered cultural and sports advantages, but there was no ice skating to school if you lived near the big lake that ended at the schoolhouse. Teachers couldn't help children identify birds and wildflowers during the sweet time of spring, and scholars couldn't swing on slender birch trees bent by the previous winter's ice storms. We could catch up on culture, but the beauty of nature, and the substantial, well-rounded education we received in our one-room school was unique. Christmas times there were to be remembered like diamonds on the heart.

May B. Davidson was born in Breman, Maine, and now lives in Round Pound. She is a former chicken farmer, sheep farmer, co-inventor of the Maine Buoy Bell, and author of the memoir, Whatever It Takes.

A Tree for the Roosevelts
1941

In the fall of 1941, a group of locals from Calais wrote President Franklin D. Roosevelt to offer him a Christmas tree cut from St. Croix Island. St. Croix Island, located in Passamaquoddy Bay just across from Calais, was the site of a French settlement in 1604. Although the settlement survived less than a year due to the extreme weather conditions, it is thought to be the site of the first observation of the Christmas holiday on western soil.

Roosevelt, charmed by the island's historical significance, accepted the gift. He returned a letter to the residents of Calais in late November, but because of how far the letter had to travel, it took several weeks to arrive. By the time the President's letter reached Calais on December 9th, the attack on Pearl Harbor only two days earlier had shaken the nation to its core.

Propelled by the excitement of having a Maine tree in the White House along with a deep sense of patriotic duty, the group from Calais quickly dispatched to St. Croix Island. They were met by Constance and Elson Small, the keepers of the island lighthouse. Constance and Elson were at first hesitant to take the eighteen-foot fir tree off the island, as there were already very few tall trees. However, the solemn events of the days prior convinced them it was the right thing to do. The tree was felled and sent to Washington.

Upon the tree's arrival in Washington, it was taken into the White House and set up in the Roosevelts' private quarters. Only a few days later Winston Churchill arrived to talk with President Roosevelt about the threats the world faced from Japan and Germany. As America braced for war, an evergreen tree from Maine watched over the Roosevelts and their family and friends as they celebrated Christmas in the wake of a national tragedy.

Maine Christmas

Rosemary Clifford Trott
1948

Fill the bowls with streaming cider,
Pile the birch logs high,
Wreathe the window frames with holly,
Let good friends stop by.

Village hills are frosted over,
Ice sheets deck the bay,
All the farm's aglow with Christmas
In the old Maine way.

Now the Grange hall sounds with laughter,
And the square's alight
As the strains of "Hail, Lord Jesus"
Echo down the night.

Yuletide Cheer and Purple Shirts
Helen Hamlin
1945

Christmas morning was bright and sunshiny on Umsaskis Lake, deep in the wilderness of Northern Maine. Frost glimmered and sparkled under sunlight, and the frost-encrusted window panes of our cabin sparkled in the brightness. My husband, Curly, a game warden, has been up early lighting both fires in the cook stove and the bulldog stove, and I heard him rummaging among the parcels we had piled up on the desk.

"No fair peeking till I get up," I called.

"You'd better get up then," he said, "I've found two neckties already."

I jumped out of bed onto the cold floor and went out into the warm kitchen. The little tree we have decorated looked quite gay in the small room. Luckily the road wasn't closed yet and we had been able to get our mail. We had quite an array of curious-looking packages piled under the tree. When Curly went out for two pails of water he called to me to come out and see the partridge.

We had seven of them in the dooryard that morning. Two of them were perched in the bare tree in front of the cabin while the others were huddled around the porch. They looked forlorn and lonesome in the white snow, and they had watched us with beady, unafraid eyes. I emptied the bread jar for them and added the few pieces of johnnycake we had left over from the night before. The partridge scuttled away when we threw it out to them, but after we were back in the camp we could watch them pecking away at the crusts.

I dressed hurriedly in my slacks and shirt so we could unwrap what Santa had brought. Curly had only two neckties this time, but he had a purplish woolen shirt with a greenish-grey plaid, an elegant Canadian dream. We had some badly needed sheets and dish towels, and Curly presented me with a pair of cream-colored mukluks with brown spots on them. I set them to soak in a pail of water to soften them and started making pies for dinner. Curly kept strutting around in his purplish shirt, getting in the way.

"Gee Pooie, where did you ever get it?"

"At Chuinards in St. Pamphile," I said. "It was the only one of its kind."

"Gee Pooie, it sure is a swell blue color."

"It's not blue. It's purple."

"Purple! Holy old Mackinaw. I can't wear a purple shirt. It's blue, isn't it?" he pleaded.

"No, it's purple."

The telephone rang two long and a short and I answered it. Anna wanted us to come up to Churchill for dinner. The Bridges and the Druins and Mr. Tarr and Miss Colson were to be there.

"What can I bring?" I asked. "I have two pies in the oven."

"We have plenty, but you can bring what you want to," Anna said.

"We'll be there."

"Where?" Curly asked.

"Churchhill, up to Deblois'. Anna wants us to come up to dinner. We'll wait for the pies and then get started."

We snowshoed out to the main road where we left our car. Two other cars had gone by since that morning, and we knew the Bridges and Druins were ahead of us. It was bright and crisp outdoors, and although the thermometer registered twenty below it didn't seem cold because the air was dry and crackling. The trees and hills were veritable Christmas cards with the blue, blue background of sky and the sunny sparkle on the snow. Curly drove along gingerly.

"One more storm will close the road."

He shifted into second to climb the long hill. The old deserted lumber camps along the road looked quite cozy under their heavy blanket of snow. It took us an hour to drive the ten miles to Churchhill. We stopped at the Giguares' cabin to see their Christmas tree and the new sleds the young sisters had. All of them were outfitted with new boots and mittens too.

"Merry Christmas!" Joe Giguare shouted, "Come in, come in. I got some potato wine. I make it last year!"

Mrs. Giguare poured us a small glass of the clear potato wine.

"*Mon Dieu!*" she exclaimed in French. "See Curly's shirt!"

"By damn me!" Joe said, "I always want a blue shirt like that!"

"It's purple." I said.

"*Mais oui,*" Mrs. Giguare said, "*C'est violette.*"

The potato wine was cold and dry tasting.

On our way to the boarding house of the Deblois' we met Mrs. Paquet with two huge thickly frosted cakes.

"Merry Christmas!" Curly nearly went off the road. "One cake for me and one for the rest of the gang!"

"All right if you can eat it all," Mrs. Paquet laughed. "Come give me a hand with these. Louis is bringing some gravy."

Everybody was in the kitchen at the boarding house.

"Merry Christmas!" they shouted.

"*Joyeuse Noel!*" Narciss Druin roared. "See the blue shirt Santa Claus bring to Curly!"

"It's red," Bridgie said.

"It's purple!" Mooney laughed.

"God's sake, Bridgie, can't you tell the difference between red and purple?"

Joe Belois was the only man there who wasn't color blind.

"He's purple," Joe affirmed. "I never see a purple shirt."

Anna and Mrs. Deblois already had the table set.

"Someone ring the gong," Anna said, "and bring the children in."

I grabbed for the big spoon. "I've always wanted to ring that thing! Let me do it!"

A feast was laid out on the long table in the kitchen and Mrs. Deblois had her best china out. There were pork roasts and chicken, mashed potatoes, gravy, Harvard beets, squash, molded salads, raised rolls, and cakes and pies. Joe Deblois brought out glasses of golden dandelion wine for everyone.

"*Mange!* Eat!"

Mrs. Deblois' cheeks were pink from the heat of the stove. None of us had to be coaxed. The children noisily settled themselves at the table while we established a plate filling brigade for them. The food was delicious and we ate until we were stuffed.

"This is the last time this Winter I'll get any cake like this," Curly said with his mouth full. "Don't forget to get some eggs, Pooie."

"I have six dozen for you," Mrs. Paquet said.

"It's going to snow for us," commented Louie.

"Did you bring your records, Mrs. Bridges?" Anna called from the other end of the table.

"Yes, sir, I sure did. Going to sashay up and sashay down once more this year. Won't get in here again this Winter."

With dinner over we washed dishes. Narciss had the phonograph going and was dancing Mrs. Deblois around the kitchen, dodging the stove and the wood box.

"Have to kiss the cook!" Narciss shouted. "Come on, Bridgie."

"We'll all kiss the cook!" Bridgie yelled. "Come on, Curly, come on, Louie!"

"*Non, non!*" Mrs. Deblois protested blushing furiously, but she was soundly kissed just the same.

We had some time to dance one "Lady of the Lake" and a "Dive and Siz" before we noticed the snow.

"Here it is," Bridgie said. "Better get your coat, Mooney, we'll have to hurry with forty-five miles ahead of us."

Everybody got ready to leave. This was the storm that would close the road for the season. The Bridges didn't linger as they had the farthest to go.

"Be sure you call us on the phone," Anna said to them, "so we'll know if you got there."

The Druins and Mr. Tarr and Miss Colson left next, and Curly and I weren't far behind them. Mrs. Paquet brought over our eggs and a large mysterious looking package.

"It's for you, Curly," she whispered. "They didn't eat it all."

"Holy smokes! Thanks!" Curly nearly burst. We said goodbye to all of them.

"See you next May," I shouted, "Merry Christmas!"

It was dark and snowing heavily by the time we parked the car in the garage at the main road and strapped on our snowshoes to go into our camp. All we could see was the white blur of the trail ahead of us. It was warmer now and the world seemed to have closed in around us. The cabin was still warm when we got inside. Curly pumped up the gasoline lantern and I turned on the radio.

"Are we going to eat?" Curly asked.

"What!" I almost shouted.

"Well, we can eat the cake," he suggested

"And coffee," I added. "Mooney should call in an hour or two."

"Ummm." Curly gingerly unwrapped his cake and stuck his finger in the frosting.

We were warm and cozy when we got the fires going again, and it was very quiet outside, a deep, peaceful, Christmas quiet. There was no frost on the window panes and we could see the soft white flakes of snow piling up on the outside sills.

Helen Hamlin was a writer and wife to a fish and game warden and lived deep in the Maine wilderness. She authored several books, including Nine Mile Bridge. *This essay originally appeared in* The Pine Cone *magazine.*

Christmas Night in Maine
Pearl LeBaron Libby
1950

Golden stars in a purple sky,
And the river deep
In its quiet sleep,
With the pines standing guard nearby.

Voices ringing so sweet and clear,
In the carols old
That each year unfold
To the wide world's listening ear.

Friendly homes with their hearth-fires bright,
Where the children play
At the close of day,
And a Christmas tree gleams with light.

Pansies for Christmas?

Rangeley Highlander
1958

This seems to be the year for June in December here in Rangeley. On December 22, Mrs. Otto Wilbur found a pansy blooming in her garden on Maine Street and sent it off to The Highlander via her grandson, Paul Hawkes. The garden, on the west side of the house, was liberally covered with snow. Then, three days of rain occurred, with temperatures between forty and fifty, the snow washed away, and out popped the pansy. Mrs. Wilbur took it in before it had time to find out that Christmas and cold weather were still ahead.

A County Tree Goes Washington
1959

In 1958, the city of Presque Isle was planning a celebration to mark the one hundred years since the city's incorporation. As part of the festivities, the city applied to Washington, D.C. to provide that year's National Christmas tree which would stand on the south lawn of the White House.

The National Christmas tree had traditionally come from a national forest west of the Mississippi, but Presque Isle was undeterred and submitted the request. In March of 1958, the city got word that they were selected to provide the Christmas tree for the 1959 Christmas celebrations in Washington.

The city set to work finding the perfect tree to present to the White House, then occupied by President Eisenhower. After searching the farms, forests, and fields of the city for months, Presque Isle and federal officials finally agreed on the perfect evergreen. Their selection was a grand, eighty-five-year-old, seventy-foot tall, white spruce from the Alice Kimball farm on Parsons Road. It took a team of five men nearly eight hours to cut the tree, bind it, and put it on a train for the eight-hundred-mile journey. Once the tree arrived at its destination it was festooned with decorations and was lit by Eisenhower at the Pageant of Peace.

The tree was the only National Christmas tree to ever come from Maine. In 1978, the tradition of sending a fresh cut tree to the White House lawn was ended when a permanent tree was planted on the south lawn.

Maine Tree Shipped to Vietnam

The Lewiston Daily Sun
1967

Governor Kenneth M. Curtis has sent a Maine Christmas tree to Vietnam at the request of an Augusta girl, Sp. 5 Ida Colford, who is now a W.AC. Secretary at U.S. Army Headquarters in Saigon. The tree is being flown from Maine to Southeast Asia via Pan American Airlines. Passage for the tree is being paid for by the state.

The tree was cut in Franklin and presented to the governor by the Maine Christmas Tree Growers Association. Maine-made ornaments for the tree were donated by Ernest Paione, president of Paragon Glass Works, Inc. of Lewiston. The tree is a nine-foot balsam fir, typical of the thousands of trees harvested each year in Maine for the Eastern Seaboard market.

It had to be specially wrapped for shipment and accompanied by instructions from Governor Curtis that it be refrigerated in Saigon until ready for use because "the needles might fall off in the warm climate if let out too soon before Christmas."

Sp. 5 Colford, who used to work for the state as a secretary, asked Governor Curtis for the tree last month in a letter.

Her request was referred to the Forestry Department and the Department of Economic Development. Everything was easy to obtain except passage to Vietnam.

Ever since the foul-up two years ago on gifts to servicemen in Vietnam that resulted in a bottleneck at the shipping point in Utah, the government has clamped down on using military transportation facilities for such ventures. Many troops are flown to Southeast Asia now via commercial jets instead of Air Force planes. With no official way to get the tree there, the State had to make other arrangements. Pan American Airlines agreed to ship it for $150.

Govenor Curtis called the combined efforts of the Maine citizens a "fitting tribute from our state during this Holiday Season. I am pleased to take a part in this effort to have a Christmas tree for our troops in the Saigon area, and I'm particularly happy to note that it is a Maine tree," he said.

In her letter to Governor Curtis, Sp. 5 Colford said she wanted a Maine tree at Army headquarters because "Maine grows the biggest and prettiest trees in the United States."

At Christmas

Doris Davis
1971

We are going to Grandma's for Christmas,
There'll be turkey and pie and a tree.
There'll be chestnuts to roast by the fire
And candy for Mollie and me.

The big tree will be in the parlor,
All covered with tinsel and toys,
With presents galore for the grown ups,
And good things for wee girls and boys.

At evening we'll sit 'round the fireplace,
To tell Christmas tales, and pop corn,
And Grandma will sing, at the organ
Of the night when the Christ Child was born.

There'll be peace and good will and contentment,
The whole house will glow with good cheer,
And when we go home, we'll be planning
On Christmas at Grandma's next year.

Christmas in Castine

Alison Wyrley Birch
1972

There are some things of value that may get lost in an age of miracles and moon probes, and one of these is Christmas in Castine. I had to go back to Maine at Christmas on a family matter for the first time in twenty-five years. It was a step backwards in time to return to the old house in a white and mysterious December. How I got there would be a story in itself, since most of the customary transportation methods aren't on schedules at this time of year. I had thought of myself as thrown against the silver sky in a shaft of steel, riding the clouds like a hopped-up Santa Claus.

But the only locomotion geared to Maine-bound travel in winter is a roadbound Greyhound bus. Mine was choosey and discriminating in the morning, only stopping at major cities like Boston and Portland on its way north from Connecticut. But once over the border in Maine, it began pausing at every cigar store, and discharging and inhaling passengers and pawing the ground like an impatient silver dinosaur.

Somewhere in the interior of Maine, a fellow traveler turned to me and spoke for the first time that day. "Are you going all the way through to Bangor?" he asked. I told him I was and he heaved a sigh and sank deeper into his seat. "God, what an experience!" he said.

All Is Calm

Having seen Maine only in the summer since I moved away, I was excited by the constant panorama, like a magnificent collection of Christmas cards. The construction of the earth was as visible as a skeleton devoid of flesh and the snow, spread in all the right places, accentuated the framework of the land. Houses, indispensable white churches and soft, yellow lights were almost too much to take. The rivers ran to the ice-clogged shores and the pine trees marched out in formation to have a look. It's easy to believe that while the rest of the world will change, Maine will continue to hold its churches in and keep its landscapes virtuous against the promises of time.

It snowed all the night I arrived in Castine. I sat with the family before the fire and listened to the storm. There's a sound to winter silence in Maine. It's as if you can hear each tender flake hit upon another. A fox barked all that night in the dark and the wind bellowed at the bay. Branches tapped against the windows and the snow kept coming down. Then the Christmas season came to Castine and it was provocative and mythical, like the true reliving of an old discarded wish. We had hot mulled cider by the gallon—a drink I hadn't tasted in years. We decked the living room with boughs of pine and hung handmade wreaths on the door. We strung white popcorn alternately with red cranberries and draped the tree with the lengths of chain as we used to do way back before the old farmhouse knew what electric lighting was.

The villagers had been invited to come to our 150 acres to hunt and pick their own Christmas trees and have a spot of cheer with us before the fire. Small bands of people, tall and short, arrived in a stream done up like Eskimos and all unrecognizable. We ploughed through acres of snow, dispersing and regrouping in the silent woods. "I've got a good one!" yelled Frank, and off we stumbled in the direction of his voice, muffled in the winter silence and in his scarf of wool.

This hooded and mittened band of foresters, with trees against their shoulders in the winter woods, tunnelled back to the house, jubilant and breathing fog. One needed a hot drink and a good fire about them. Christmas took on the shape and fragrance of tradition while people shouted "Merry Christmas!" out of their hooded heads, and strapped Christmas trees to the roofs of station wagons and jeeps and burrowed back through the snow that the wind reshaped with a cold but kindly hand, back to their own holiday hearths.

If it hadn't snowed perhaps I wouldn't have been so filled with nostalgia and maybe hot mulled cider isn't all that good. I didn't find the fox that had barked his message at the night, but I found his footprints in the snow and met head on a startled white cat that had taken squatter's rights to our old barn. Like a huge and angry snowball, he bolted out of the hay loft, a winter white, all but the angry eyes.

Christmas on an old Maine farm has to take these beasts in its stride, and it's all to the good to know that real animals have certain housing privileges in this white and frosty retreat. I was tempted to check the roof for reindeer footprints, since nostalgia took on such a third-dimensional proportion here they seemed a possibility.

I went back to Connecticut in time for our own tinsel and electric lights brilliantly spanning an all-aluminum tree. There's a lot to be said for progress. I like it a lot. But Christmas in Castine, just now and then, has something to do, I believe, with the balance of Nature.

While the Village Sleeps

Jan Thompson
1971

Twilight and a multitude
Of stars find the
Little village nestled
In the mountains
Fast asleep…

Fluffy gray clouds
Slipping quietly
Over the horizon
And the stars silently
Fade away . . .

The sun slowly rises
Awakening the valley
To a land transformed
By the glistening
White snow . . .

The "Used-to-Be" Christmas
Lavina P. Walker
1973

The house wasn't much. Over a hundred years old, it looked every day of it. I remember seeing it once, an elegant patrician lady poised on the hilltop gowned in fresh summer yellow paint, but usually it was weather-beaten. It would have been a misfit anywhere in the world except where it was—out in the boonies up in Maine. The road approaching it wasn't too much more than a cow path.

The walk to the mailbox each day, though usually fruitless, was invigorating. Both ways, it was a mile; and the way back was a steep climb, but the view from the kitchen window was worth every step of it. When the owner was asked how much land he possessed, he had to confess that he really didn't know—"'bout as fer as you can see." You could see forever.

The main house was a giant set amidst the barns and chicken houses, a pig shelter, and a motley assortment of various other out-buildings. Everything peered out from under mountains of sugar-white snow, looking like a frightfully expensive painting. Tall, graceful evergreens with white frosting composed the frame as if protecting "the farm." From what? The future and its progress, perhaps.

When one entered the house, a blast of cold air hurtled through the high-ceilinged rooms and was chased into the corners by the roaring heat from a glossy black woodstove where coffee perked an incessant jig. The air was permeated by the smell of good things to eat which lined the stove and table and seemingly miles of sideboards.

In back of the country kitchen, the size of a modern-day house, lay a spacious living room where a sparkling fire burned robustly in the fireplace and a huge Christmas tree clamored for domination of the room. Gay Christmas packages littered everywhere composed the only color scheme.

The house was not modern, but it was big and rambling and capable of stretching itself to accommodate the dozen children, hordes of grandchildren, and gradually great-grandchildren who returned to be enfolded by its warmth each year at Christmas.

Little ones wore faces scrubbed Sunday school clean, but no amount of rubbing could erase the pinkish glow of excitement—excitement stemming from a Santa who made children jubilant with practical, sturdy new clothes, a few home-made toys, and perhaps a smattering of dime store stuff.

There was a constant peering out of windows into the ebony of night powered with falling snow for late arrivals who came from as far away as Boston. Hugging and kissing and squeezing of each newly arrived relative made breathing delightfully impossible. New babies created a frenzy of ooh's and aah's and oh's and were passed from arm to arm and back again. Reverent prayers were said for those departed, and family skeletons emerged from hidden closets in whispered secrecy not a breath later. The air was filled with many things—but mostly with the laughter of love, love of family, friends, fellow man, and God.

Strangers now own this old house. It is gone to its family forever, but only in reality. And in reality people are digging through attics of trash and retrieving its treasures. Hopefully they will discover one of the most glorious treasures of all, the used-to-be Christmas.

Christmas Reunion
Doris Barbour Jordan
1972

The log is alight, the tree is bright,
Lips are gay with laughter;
Love abounds and song resounds
From every beam and rafter;
The feast is spread and every head
Is bowed in sweet communion,
Let each one here in silent prayer
Give thanks for this reunion;
And let the prayers speed far and wide
For Peace this joyous Christmastide.

First Christmas as Maine Homeowners

A. Carman Clark

1973

Have you ever received a bag of onions as a Christmas gift? Not any old onions, but firm white ones, dried in the barn chamber, sorted by work-calloused hands, and presented with pride so that the holiday dinner vegetable, dripping with cream and butter, would be top quality onions—all of a size.

Our neighbors spread our festive board for our first Christmas in Maine. They came to our door with gifts from their kitchens and garden to welcome us to their lake-filled valley and to personally extend holiday greetings. When I look back, now, to my surprise and pleasure at this country Christmas custom, I find a happy jumble of memories tinged with new tastes and smells. Each neighbor family brought with their gift of friendship some product of their own harvest or culinary talents.

The onions were wonderful—firm, sweet, and full of flavor. There were jars of rhubarb conserve, the tartness of the early spring stalks accented with slivers of orange peel and the richness of walnuts. The glasses of chokecherry jelly were a vibrant red in color, sharp and sweet in taste. Swedish curl cookies, delicate, mildly sweet, deftly cooled over the long handle of a wood spoon, were a contrast to the rich Scotch shortbread and the chocolate caramels, all gifts from different kitchens with good Maine cooks.

Almost too lovely to use was a demure, old-fashioned girl carved in fresh, home-made butter, a gift from a neighbor with artistic fingers, a warm heart, and good cows. Finnish coffee buns, tender, light, yeast dough, flavored with cardamom seeds, brought us our first taste of this coffee-break treat which is so popular in this area.

There were baskets of yellow and red apples, polished and shining with best wishes ". . . from our orchard to your table." The dark fruit cake had been made by our local postal clerk before the rush season and stored to increase the spicy richness of flavor. The popcorn balls were made on a Sunday by a busy storekeeper. The sour pickles—called Saturday night pickles because they go so well with Downeast baked beans—had been canned on a warm August evening.

Maine tarts, a cross between shortcake and pie pastry, were brought with jars of apple and crabapple jelly. Venison mincemeat and maple syrup added variety to our gifts and a conversation point for learning more about our new neighbors.

We have learned to make these foods which came to us that Christmas as gifts, for sharing recipes enlarges friendships. But each one still belongs, in our associations, with those Maine people who welcomed us and said their "Merry Christmas" as they spread our festive board. A bag of onions, or a crock of mincemeat, a plate of cookies or a butter statue . . . the gifts were individual, delicious and delightful. This Maine custom we will help preserve and perpetuate.

Sharing Christmas

Beatrice Comas
1974

Have you ever gone Christmas shopping with your "best friend"? And, why do other people's errands always seem more fascinating than your own? We first stopped at a shop that specializes in all sorts of elegant bathroom accessories, such as squishy, cushioned toilet seats. I had never before sat on a lucite seat with a small fortune of shiny coins encased within. My friend chose one in white patent leather and had it put on "layaway" to allow time for a friend or relative to take the hint and buy it for her. Though expensive, such an indulgence is a good bargain in the end because it transforms necessity into lingering luxury.

Next we stopped at a pet supply store for some catnip toys for one of her friends who owns three cats, although no one ever really owns a cat. Even old cats are temporarily rejuvenated by a few sniffs of catnip.

One more errand to a busy and famous hamburger outlet for a book of gift certificates. These were not for me, as I had hoped, but for a pampered poodle who lives in Florida, has her nails manicured and painted weekly, and wears a collar of genuine turquoise. Since this little snob usually dines on the same gourmet fare as her mistress, she occasionally likes to "go slumming." If Princess Grace has the chance, wouldn't she enjoy a "Dunkin' Donut"? This little prin-cess eats only the meat filling so her owner has a weight problem from eating too many buns.

What about *my* Christmas list? It's still in my pocketbook, but I did get something I hadn't bargained for . . . a Christmas cold. That is what you get for wearing your outdoor clothes indoors, or when your resistance is lowered from too much Yuletide shopping.

There are a number of things in which I have lost faith in 1974, but I believed, or wanted to, that dental cavities and the common cold could never afflict anyone past fifty. I had counted on this as a bonus for my old age. A common cold seems very un-common when it happens to you, but as "common" means "belonging equally to, or shared by everyone or all," it is an accurate all-encompassing diagno-sis. As for sharing, no doubt some unsuspecting shopper on whom I may have sneezed in the bargain basement is cursing her share.

I awoke "the morning after" with my face puffed and mottled with fever. My eyes were two red, watery slits. I can neither taste nor smell and have no desire to get dressed or even go near a store. As if that weren't bad enough, I think I am allergic to the plastic Christ-mas tree which my clever spouse finally assembled.

Hark, do I hear him gargling? Could it be I have "shared" my cold with him?

Christmas morning may dawn clear and white, but for us it will be sneezy, queasy, and blue. Our gifts to each other? Industrial size cases of paper hankies. Never mind what color!

A Tree Full of Memories

Bill Caldwell, Maine Sunday Telegram
1978

In almost every home today, Maine families are probably enjoying some special family ceremony that, more than anything else, spells Christmas to them. Usually it's something small, something a bit strange to outsiders—but very special to the family.

In our house it's the last box of special ornaments left—pass alongs from generations ago, survivors for up to 150 years. Or they are primitive ornaments, made in remote villages of distant countries and carried home to the States to brighten up our tree: sweet alien notes signifying ties to a village in Cambodia, a temple in Siam, a minaret in Constantinople, the Wailing Wall in Israel.

We hang these ornaments last, partly to save them from the perils of Piper, the dalmation with the side-wiping tail; Dickens, the lightning-fast undersized coon cat; and Ski, the haughty elder-statesman of a cat, bossy in his marmalade coat. This trio erupts into wild steeplechases around and through every Christmas tree, causing more havoc in two seconds than a Maine tornado.

The reason we hang this special box of ornaments last is because they are memories more than they are ornaments. To hang memories requires time that moves slowly, as on Christmas Eve, and gentle, unrushed hands. It also requires a very tolerant audience of one—to wit, my two-year-old granddaughter, Chiloe, who has charm, interest, patience and laughing, loving eyes.

She unwraps the crinkled newspaper, slowly pulls away the soft tissue paper—and there is the tiger, and the elephant, and the lions, and the zebra, and the giraffe with the endless neck.

Chiloe squeals happily at each. And in a flash my mind leaps from Maine to a village in Bengal, and I can feel the heat and sniff the strong smells of the tent where these wooden animals were carved. While Chiloe hangs her tiger, that Indian hamlet and this Maine village are blended on the eve of Christmas.

Next, out of a tiny box, come milkweed pods, sliced in halves, inside each half a tiny angel. And I tell Chiloe about the little church in Bristol Mills which lost its belfry and where the ladies made quilts and toys and milkweed angels to raise the money for a new steeple. I promise to take her to that church for the bell ringing and the carol singing.

Tiny hands, remarkably gentle, unwrap a miniature Chinese dancer's hat: tall, white, papier-mache grasshoppers and brilliant-hued jungle birds from Thailand. And fat carp, fish for holiness and fertility and luck. And Chiloe hangs these Buddhist symbols amid her angels and her Santa Claus.

Now her little hands unwrap miniature temple hats, then rice baskets and tiny bamboo balls. And memories flood into this Maine house.

These ornaments were a present from a rice-planting lady and her four children in the Delta of Vietnam. They survived the war itself, but I have since heard that the mother died and two children—now about sixteen years old—were among the "boat people" to escape

Vietnam without, however, finding a haven that would allow them ashore from their leaking craft.

Chiloe hangs the rice basket and tosses the balls in happy laughter for Dickens, the miniature coon cat. I tell her no history here. Her father fought there and he has told her none.

A happy, gurgling shout of soprano pleasure and Chiloe pulls out fish dolls and cow dolls and turtle dolls from Guatemala—brilliant oranges and purples and yellows and red, sent to us by friends.

She scoffs at the next dull Christmas ornaments. But I fondle these old, sacred, cheap-stuff friends. These are the survivors of the ornaments Barbara and I bought together for our first Christmas of marriage, in New York City in 1944.

Ours was a wartime marriage. I was back from Guadalcanal, not long out of the military hospitals. Storekeepers would tell me, "No ornaments for Christmas trees—no material to make them. Don't you know there's a war on?" We made do with shoddy plastics whose thin, cheap, paint has chipped away. I hang them with joy now.

Next come some heavy ornaments. The good old, solid mirror glass of grandmother's time and earlier. The tree boughs bend under these century-old ornaments that put to shame what we make today.

Now, wooden cutouts of toy soldiers, their fixed grins and colorful uniforms brilliantly painted. And again memories flood in. My daughter Susan made these for the tree when we were running a newspaper in London and she was attending an English boarding school. I see her bringing home these toys—a tiny blonde in gray flannel coat and hat, the uniform of English schoolgirls.

We hang them next to a partridge in a pear tree.

Chiloe shrieks with laughter as she pulls out the long-tailed Christmas mice. I had forgotten them until this moment: good luck mice made of red flannel, with long, long tails. And I remember now the very pretty debutante (they had such creatures in London in 1960) next door who made these little mice for her Irish Guard escorts, who wore them at parties, hung by a paper clip to the epaulettes of their splendid uniforms. And what a way for them to end up—here in a Maine winter.

The next package is another sad one: camels, wise men, shepherds tending their flock—all handsomely carved and bought from a shop in the old city of Jerusalem within earshot of the Wailing Wall. I arrange them tenderly at the foot of the tree and feel a surge of love for that magic city and hope that peace may soon envelope her.

Chiloe leaps up, dancing. She is holding some tiny brass temple bells from India and Siam whose lovely, pure liquid sounds brings back the sounds of the bells being rung by saffron-robed, shaven-headed monks in gaudy Buddhist temple courtyards. Chiloe dances to their sound today in Maine.

From a special box we unwrap the old wooden angel choir and orchestra, carved long ago in the Black Forest of Germany by a Bavarian wood cutter. With these jewel-like figures are some heavy, waxed German Christmas tree balls, embossed with gold and blue and red crosses and crowns.

Finally, the creche figures, made for Chiloe's great-great grandfather, made in Vermont. Survivors of 150 Christmases and as many children Chiloe's age. We place them around the tree.

The special box is empty now. And you would have to look carefully to find most of these last ornaments we hang hung, because so many other lights and brilliant pretties are also on the tree.

But I know, you know, and now Chiloe knows about the most important part of the Christmas tree—the memories and joys and hopes that lie in every branch, hard to see, but filling to the heart.

Merry, happy Christmas.

Christmas on an Island
Katherine W. Stewart
1972

At Christmas on our island, away from the marts of trade,
Away from the sorry spectacle which greed of man has made
Of what was once a time to stop and praise the Savior's Birth
We pause to offer up our prayer for lasting "Peace on Earth";
For here there's brooding quiet and we observe the Day
In reverence and deep respect in the old-fashioned way;
Christmas . . . on an island . . . Down in Maine.

An Island Christmas
Dean Lunt
Remembering 1978

In the 1970s, Frenchboro, as it had for decades, remained a relatively poor island fishing village eight miles at sea that, given the small boats and poor communications of the era, seemed especially remote and isolated during winter. That unchangeable reality of nature and geography made Christmas an especially wondrous holiday, a final burst of color and light and fun and good spirits at the hard edge of a long, dark, cold season out on the stormy Atlantic.

Like a classic play, our holiday season played out in three acts: Hopes and Dreams; Preparations; and Christmas itself. We did not live in a time or place of significant year-long gift giving—there was neither the money nor the tradition. Rather the giving of gifts— from the necessary to the practical to the fun—was largely clustered into this single holiday, only elevating its significance and anticipation in many ways regardless of age. I have no doubt that for some of my great aunts and uncles and older island neighbors, sometimes the only gifts they received the entire year were unwrapped at Christmas.

As the warm winds of summer swung to the clearing and crisp northwest winds of fall, the holiday season's opening act, as in many rural communities across America, featured the arrival of the *Sears*

Wish Book. We had no Amazon, no superstores, and no internet (we didn't have telephone service off the island until I was seventeen and the state ferry only came twice each week), so it was the annual catalog that provided the images for every kid's fantasy in full color— page after page after page of must-have presents. Here could be found the Evel Knievel Stunt Cycle, Super Toe, Electronic Slot Cars, Mattel Electronic Football, Hot Wheels, Pong, Six Million Dollar Man action figures, Rock 'Em Sock 'Em Robots, Lite Brite, Daisy BB Guns, leather footballs, Boston Red Sox pajamas, and so much more. It offered the same fantasy wonderland for adults with items ranging from dresses to work pants to appliances to tool sets to complete houses, yes, houses. It is hard to overemphasize the sheer importance of Sears to remote communities during the twentieth century.

Once the catalog arrived in the mail (our mail arrived via a daily mail boat), we circled every item we wanted, and, well, we wanted a lot. Clearly we were still jacked up on Halloween candy to believe we might get more than one of the items circled, but it was a glorious time of dreaming and agonizing over what to circle. I took it seriously enough that if I changed my mind, I noted it on the page as if fine-tuning or streamlining my requests might make a difference in what I actually received.

Once we carefully delivered the dog-eared, annotated *Wish Book* to Mom as if it were some ancient biblical scroll, Christmas as a commercial enterprise took a backseat to the dying days of fall, the first snow, and Thanksgiving before re-emerging as the centerpiece of our daily lives, except now less commercially driven and more based on community and traditions. Into the 1970s, especially in Maine's rural communities, Christmas remained an important part of school life. In fact, on Frenchboro, the island schoolteacher still doubled as the island minister until 1969 (they were called teacher-preachers). We decorated our classroom with construction paper chains and Christmas trees, and we colored nativity scenes, Santa Claus, and the three wisemen right along with completing our math worksheets and science pages. And we all practiced for the school Christmas play, a highly anticipated event that took place at the island church just a stone's throw away. The only time I have ever stepped onto a stage in costume was as an elementary school pupil in that 1890 chapel playing the Ghost of Christmas Past and assorted other characters over the years. It all felt so big! After the performance, gifts were handed out, Santa made an early island appearance, and carols were sung.

During the same time, I dug out and played our Christmas albums (*Christmas with the Chipmunks! Burl Ives Have a Holly Jolly Christmas!*) and religiously read the *TV Guide* each week to scout out favorite Christmas specials. After all, back then we only had one shot a year to watch Frosty and Rudolph and Charlie Brown. Also part of my regular viewing as a child was the local Santa Claus show on Bangor's WABI-TV each afternoon, always hoping the big man would read my name off his critical list of good boys and girls. I can't remember if he ever did, but I certainly raced from the dinner table when he was reading those names from his big book.

Outside Christmas lights were also a big deal. Islanders strung them along rooftops, along fences, and across hedges and wrapped them around outside trees. My grandparents took a ride each night after supper to see the lights. If someone was off island, they might even ask a friend to plug in their Christmas lights while they were gone to help fill the evenings with color. It was regularly reported who put them out and who did a great job, and we were more than a bit annoyed at anyone who didn't at least put electric candles in the windows. I mean, come on!

Perhaps the most enduring tradition was finding a Christmas tree. My grandmother Vivian, who loved the holiday, started searching for her tree during her summer walks, tying string around promising candidates and memorizing their location. The island features mostly older trees and ratty small spruce, but back then there remained just enough clearings and unfiltered sunlight to develop scattered small fir groves—the Holy Grail of island Christmas trees. To be clear, we are not talking bushy, full trees here; rather we only hoped to find a properly shaped tree with at least four good rows of branches on which to hang ornaments. My grandmother sometimes cheated and added a fake branch to fill out a row if necessary, but I wanted a tree not cosmetically enhanced. There were years, even as a nine- or ten-year-old, that I walked for miles zigzagging through the woods looking for the right tree. My father suffered from the delusion that any tree looked good when decorated. As if! I may have worshipped him, but from a young age I did not trust his Christmas tree instincts—At. All.—So he was relegated to putting it in the stand and stringing the lights. Even as an adult (although now I prefer very full trees), I might walk every row of live trees at Christmas tree farms throughout New England and leave empty-handed. Spindly doesn't begin to describe even the good trees we found on the island, but with enough old-fashioned silver tinsel, Angel Hair, garlands, and glass ornaments, it did sparkle. Still, each December, that first night when the scent of Balsam wafts through the house evokes childhood memories.

Once our tree was up, usually right after my brother Dave's December 18 birthday, the pile of wrapped presents slowly grew as did the temptation to shake, rattle, and roll each one. It was a long, agonizing week.

The island tradition was to open presents (or "pick the tree") from relatives on Christmas Eve and then during the night Santa came to fill stockings and leave a gift or two for Christmas morning. Frenchboro only had one mile of paved road. Given how many relatives lived within a half mile or so, on Christmas Eve we walked from house to house singing carols and watching each family open their presents, leaving the house with the youngest children for last (so they didn't have to leave their new toys behind). At the very least, we watched my grandparents, Aunt Lillian and Uncle Cecil, and Uncle John and Aunt Rebecca open presents. But in some family photos and home movies, there are a couple dozen islanders watching the festivities at each house as wrapping paper was saved, homemade snacks were served, and stories about each present and the process of finding it were shared. Many islanders carefully arranged their unwrapped presents under the tree for a day or two because people visited each other to see what was received.

It was a remarkable old-fashioned holiday and tradition that was always over too soon. One of the saddest sights I remember as a child was that undecorated, naked tree, with a few lonely strands of tinsel still clinging to branches, suddenly and unceremoniously tossed into the backyard. It meant that not only was the next Christmas a full year away, but the long, cold winter had officially arrived.

Dean Lunt, who was raised on Frenchboro, is a former journalist, founder of Islandport Press, and author of two books, including Hauling By Hand.

Winter Comes to Maine
The Maine Seacoast Missionary Society
1979

After the summer people leave, after the tourists depart, after the birds have flown south—then the winter comes to Maine. And winter in Maine is long, bleak, cold, snowy, and icy. It is common for the first snowfall to come in October and for the last snowfall to come in May. And there is always the "old-timer" who will tell about the year that snow fell on the Fourth of July!

Long, bleak, cold, snow, and icy winters are not just unpleasant; they make life difficult even for the most loyal Mainers. The difficulty of keeping warm, the difficulty of getting around, and the difficulty of just earning a living make life hard. This is why the Maine Seacoast Mission does more work in the winter than in the summer. From time to time, someone "from away" will ask, "When do you put the *Sunbeam* up for the winter?" And so we show that the winter is the *Sunbeam's* busiest and most important time of the year.

Christmas in Maine means a respite from the unpleasantness of winter. Noses may glow from the cold, but so can hearts. The snow falls to cover the ravages of the storms with a blanket of pure white. And lives, too, get another chance to improve—not only the outer appearance but the innermost being.

Where does the Mission's Christmas begin? It begins in a thousand places—in small island homes and smaller Down East houses, in small one-room schools and smaller one-room chapels, in Coast Guard barracks and in nursing homes. It begins where there is a need for something extra, and that something extra the Seacoast Mission provides makes Christmas just a little happier, just a little brighter.

From all parts of our great country come the gifts that will make Christmas brighter in Maine. Gifts of money (checks, money orders, cash) for the Christmas and Relief Fun, gifts of toys and games, gifts of knitted goods (the backbone of our Christmas giving) come in all year round. So many gifts come in December after the gifts for that year have been packed that they have to be kept for the next year. This is why we say that the Christmas season for the Maine Seacoast Mission is thirteen months long!

"Santa's Domain" is the territory of our Chief Elf, Jack Drake. Assistant Superintendent John E. Drake, to be formal, has been a member of the Mission staff since 1967. It is his job to gather the names of all those thousands who can use something extra at Christmas. And Jack has a lot of helpers—ministers and field agents of the Mission, social directors of nursing homes, and morale officers of Coast Guard bases, and contacts in small Down East hamlets and smaller island communities. This is a tremendous task since each of what will be over 2,400 gifts is for a certain individual. Each gift is wrapped for the one person known by name, by address, by age, by sex, and when possible, by what that person wants for Christmas.

The gift for a child is a box of candy, something warm to wear (mittens, muffler, cap), and something fun (a toy, a game, or a book)—all wrapped up in white with a red string. A gift for a nursing home patient may be a ditty bag stuffed with a lap robe, a box of tissues, a bottle of lotion, a box of candy, and something personal. A gift for a Coast Guard officer is our way of trying to say "thank you" for those who help the people who live by the sea.

Once the 2,400 gifts have all been selected, wrapped in white paper and tied with red string, and marked with the name of one who will be getting it, all of these must be delivered. From Mission House in Bar Harbor they go—by car, by truck, by mail, and by boat. Let us follow one gift and see it delivered.

As early in December as possible, all the gifts that are going on the *Sunbeam* will have been packed. Boat Minister Stan Haskell will load them aboard the *Sunbeam* at her berth in Northeast Harbor and, on some nice wintry day, set sail. This special Christmas trip of the *Sunbeam* will take her to all the islands served by the Sea Coast Mission—Islesford, Great Cranberry, Placentia, Frenchboro, Isle au Haut, Eagle, and Matinicus. On the other Mission islands—Swans Island, Vinalhaven, North Haven, and Islesboro—the Mission's resident minister will have the pleasant duty of serving as Santa Claus' helper.

"Getting there is half the fun"—sometimes, but not always. But early December winter has come to Maine, and with it comes the cold and the snow. On one such visit to an isolated island Stan had to go not only by *Sunbeam* but by our very small boat called a "pram" to get ashore. Since there are no paved roads, no snowplow, no four-wheel-drive vehicles, his next mode of transportation is the snowshoe. Strapping the snowshoes on his feet, he takes off through the wood to the house on the hill in the middle of the island.

Because the *Sunbeam* cannot be on every island on Christmas Day or Eve, Boat Minister Stan Haskell simply declares that the day the *Sunbeam* is there to be that island's Christmas Day! The islanders gather in church or on the *Sunbeam* to celebrate—the worship, song, gifts, happiness, mirth, joy! To provide worship for the islands is one of the most important reasons the Mission and the *Sunbeam* exist. To provide the happy worship of Christmas is the bonus!

The Mission's Christmas program not only means over 2,400 people will receive gifts, but it also means that over 1,000 children and adults will enjoy a party financed in part by the Seacoast Mission. On a dozen islands and as many Down East places there will be such a happy event sometime in mid-December. Some common meeting site—the church or chapel, the school or the town hall—will come alive with the laughter of Christmas. Hot cocoa for the kids and hot coffee for the grown-ups, and umpteen kinds of cookies, cakes, and other goodies will warm the bodies in from the bitter cold. Games, songs, and fun-time will lighten the spirits of all. And, of course, a visit from Santa Claus to give out the gifts.

The Sunbeam is operated by The Maine Seacoast Mission, a non-profit organization that serves rural and island communities in Maine. For more than a century, the Mission has delivered Christmas presents to island residents, lighthouse keepers, and now residents of Hancock and Washington counties. Much like in 1979, children still receive hats, mittens, and toys while elderly residents receive toiletries, lap robes, and books. While they no longer give out candy, the Mission still wraps its more than 1,500 gifts in their signature white butcher paper tied with red string. This essay was abridged from the society's winter 1979 newsletter.

Christmas on Naskeag Point
Roy Barrette
1981

In most of the country, about Thanksgiving Day, the first vagrant airs of approaching Christmas are witnessed to by the swaying of colored lights strung by utility company crews across High Street, Broad Street, Main Street, or whatever the principal business thoroughfare in your town is called. In my youth Thanksgiving Day was an occasion when family members gathered together and ate themselves into a semicomatose condition after they had attended church. The church service got them in the mood as the altar steps were piled high with all the brightly colored fruits of the field and garden. Nowadays, Thanksgiving seems to have been jockeyed by chambers of commerce into the position of lead horse for a continuous spending spree stretching from late November until after New Year's.

Where I live, happily, it is not quite that way. Not yet anyway. Here, the first signs of Christmas may be detected in the sudden appearance of ancient trucks piled high with undecorated Christmas wreaths lurching around the corners of the narrow roads. Or the load may be simply brush headed for somebody's dooryard where it will serve as a supply depot for the members of the family who are engaged in "wreathing."

All Is Calm

Wreathing is not a pastime for pale hands, pink tipped and certainly not in a class with embroidery, or making lavender sachets out of odd pieces of silk rescued from the ragbag. The work begins by getting brush out of the woods, which is a cold, sticky, rough job. Experienced wreathers say the spills (which is what the needles are called hereabouts) stay on longer if the brush has been subjected to a couple of frosts. Sometimes the frost turns into snow, which makes the work tougher, and lugging the brush out of the car or truck calls for strength and sure-footedness. Our woods are not like the Black Forest, all combed and orderly. I usually allow my neighbors to cut brush on my place which, except for the fields someone cleared by hand long ago (and one I cleared more recently with a bulldozer), is pretty much as the last ice age left it, studded with boulders as big as a henhouse down to little ones perfectly calculated to cause you to slip and break your ankle.

Balsam fir wreaths are preferable to those made of spruce. They smell better and the needles hang on longer. The fragrance is the thing, though. I send a few south to my unfortunate friends who live in Florida in the winter and the first comment in their "thank you" letter is that they were enveloped by the fragrance of the Maine woods the moment they opened the box. Houses where wreaths are made are filled with the odor of balsam too, but they are filled with something else, and that is, spills. After you have put together a few hundred wreaths on the living room floor you will find needles still around when you do your spring cleaning.

Out here on Naskeag Point and in a hundred remote "Dunnett Landings" (remember Sarah Orne Jewett and *The Country of the*

Pointed Firs?) like it along the coast of Maine, we escape the commercialization of Christmas to a great degree. I don't claim we are as we were two-hundred years ago when Saddrach Watson ran his store here on "The Point," and presumably sold rum to the Indians, but there are no more houses or people than there were one hundred years ago. True, we now have to go fifteen miles to Blue Hill to buy our rum, but we make do, and there are still a few apples around if you enjoy a slice of apple floating on the top of your steaming hot toddy.

I don't know of any great lighting displays, though most houses have a few candles in the windows. Twenty years ago, shortly after I came here, I lugged a ten-foot spruce tree in from the woods and planted it between my house and the barn. For a long time I decorated it with colored lights at Christmas. As the years slipped by, I found I needed extra strings of lights until finally I accumulated eight or ten. Decorating that old skunk spruce got to be quite a chore, but I kept it up because my neighbors in the village brought kids down on the crisp winter nights to gaze upon its fountain of color. You have all heard the story of the boy who lifted a calf every day on the theory he could keep it up indefinitely as he would grow stronger as the calf grew bigger. It didn't work out that way. The calf grew bigger faster than he grew stronger. Finally my spruce did that too. It is not as tall as a redwood, but I now have to look up at it from my bedroom window. The only way I could string lights on it would be by getting the fire laddies to do the job. They would, I am sure. I am the one who gave up. Now I have a dozen wreaths all gay with red ribbons on the panels of my white picket fence. True, you can't see them at night except as they show up in the headlights of your car, but people enjoy them during the daytime and that is what Christmas decorations are for, isn't it?

Years ago, when my grandchildren were little (they are grown now with children of their own), they used to come to Maine for the holidays and I always took them to the barn on Christmas Eve. There is something particularly appealing, even to non-Christians, about the story of the Christ child lying in a manger. I guess there is not much of a difference between my barn on Naskeag Point and the one in Galilee two-thousand years ago. Joseph would recognize it for what it is. Family barns (not big commercial establishments) are pretty much the same all over the world. There is the same hollow sounds of stamping feet on the barn floor as you open the door; the same scrambling as the cows rise to greet you; and the same barn smell, that may be offensive to some, but is a pleasant thing to a farmer. People who work the land are alike too. I have a better understanding of a smallholder in England, or a Central American Indian plowing his rocky hillside with a crooked stick than I do of a city man in London with his striped pants and a top hat, or a trader on the floor of the stock exchange in New York.

My purpose in getting the kids to the barn on Christmas Eve was so they could see the cows kneel to the Savior as they do, momentarily, when they rise clumsily to their feet, hind legs first. It was always so mysterious; the dark, shadowy, cobwebby barn, with just a little hay dust shimmering in the air. I always took an old-fashioned lantern with me (a flashlight as a spare) and hung the lamp on the same hook as my predecessors in office had hung theirs on a hundred years ago. There were deep shadows in the corners and when I said, "Be quiet!" the only sounds were those of the breathing of the animals and their restless movements. My cows are gone now but the barn remains awaiting new occupants. Everything else is the same, and who knows, if the world continues on its present course, we may all be glad to get back to the times when eggs came from the henhouse, milk from the family cow, and wool from one's sheep.

There are no stores around the corner in our rural community, but my neighbors do take their kids to the "city" (Ellsworth, population 5,000) for a little Christmas shopping. They don't go often, no more than a couple of times. A Christmas shopping spree is still an adventure. They set off with Mother—Father is usually working—and make a day of it. They have lunch (a hamburger or a hot dog, or a pizza, of course) in one of the half-a-dozen eateries; make forays into all the shops, each time piling their purchases in the back of the car; and finally, everybody tired and all their money gone, make their way home thirty or forty miles in the early darkness which falls here by four o'clock at Christmas. On the drive home they pass houses, far spaced for the most part, which have a few Christmas lights swaying from little trees to be glimpsed through the small-paned windows. In Maine you don't need a large display to let the world know what is in your heart. There are no spectaculars like the Rockefeller Center tree or the one on the White House lawn. The few beckoning red or green flashes, blinking in the windy darkness like the running lights on ships, carry the message just as well.

I will never forget the evening when my wife and I drove to Stonington to attend a joint meeting of school committee members. It had been a stormy week and the forecast was snow for Christmas. For the benefit of those unfamiliar with our local geography, Stonington can be described as a Maine coastal village—working not tourist—built on a solid granite hillside that pitches steeply down to the harbor. To get to it from the mainland you must cross a high bridge over

Eggemoggin Reach onto Little Deer Isle, then over a long causeway not much above sea level to Deer Isle, then the full length of the island to where Stonington looks out over a gaggle of small islands to Isle au Haut and the Atlantic Ocean.

It was dark when we started, but we had no trouble until we reached the causeway, which had been flooded at high water. The ebbing tide had left ice floes here and there the whole length of the road. Already a truck was using its snowplow to shove the larger pieces back into the ocean. The chore was not a straightforward job because the causeway is lined each side with big granite boulders and the floes had to be eased through the open spaces between them. Anyway, with ingenuity and patience we got across. It took a while and the car was not too warm, but when we climbed the hill on Deer Isle and I began to see candles in the windows and a few colored lights here and there, I felt rewarded for our efforts. The moon came out, too, and I have seldom seen anything more beautiful than the combination of twinkling lights, dark water covered with ice floes, and the high bridge silhouetted against a sky of hurrying broken clouds.

I am going back for another look this Christmas. A new Christmas, but the enchantment will be the same. The moon and the ice floes have been around since the memory of man runneth not to the contrary, older than Christmas, and are about as close as I shall come to touching the hem of the robe of immortality.

Ray Barrette was a columnist, author, and writer who lived on Amen Farm in Brooklin. This essay orginally appeared in Down East *magazine.*

Launching a Holiday Tradition

Trudy Chambers Price

Remembering 1984

It was my idea to put a lighted tree on top of the seventy-foot Harvestore silo on our 150-acre dairy farm in Knox, Maine. I thought something so out of the ordinary would surely liven up the holiday season, and it was an inexpensive way to cheer people. My family was not so thrilled with the idea.

The little girl in me still found magic in holiday lights. I loved getting the tree into the house early so I could enjoy it for several weeks before Christmas. I'd lie on the couch and dream back to when I knew for certain there would be a new doll under the tree—every single Christmas until I was fifteen. For me, the tree lost its magic as soon as the gifts were opened, although I kept it in the house well into January. And now, the idea of a lighted tree on top of the silo—awesome!

After suggesting several more times that we put a tree on the silo, Ron and the boys finally agreed to do it if I would help.

"I'll buy the lights and help pick out a tree," I said enthusiastically.

"That's not the sort of help we had in mind," Ron replied. "We want you to actually help put the tree up there."

"You mean climb up the silo?" I asked. They nodded in unison.

They knew I was afraid of heights. They'd been trying for years to get me up on that silo but I had no desire to do so. In the fall, after the silo was full, someone had to climb to the top and sweep off the haylage that accumulated as it was blown into the top pipe (this was basically for aesthetics—there was no actual need to do this). I couldn't even watch as Ron, Kyle, or Travis, tied with a rope from his waist to the rail around the catwalk, walked out onto the slanted silo top and swept it clean, let alone do it myself.

"Mom, you would be so glad if you did it," Kyle coaxed. "The view is great. You can see all around for miles. Come on, won't you?"

"No, I won't," I replied, "and I'll take your word about the view. Besides, I think it's mean of you to try to bribe me just because you know how much I want a tree up there."

"Think of it as a challenge," Ron said.

I thought about the tree for several days. Then I purchased the lights—four strings of twenty-five each. At supper I announced that I had bought the lights and that I would help put up the tree. They seemed surprised and I'm not certain they believed me. Secretly I thought that surely if they took time to cut a tree and I helped with the preparations, they wouldn't back out at the last minute if I refused to climb the silo. Would they?

When my parents arrived for Thanksgiving, I told them about our plan.

"Quite an ambitious project, isn't it?" my father asked. I knew by his voice that the idea intrigued him.

After Thanksgiving dinner, we went to the pasture and chose a large tree. Then, with my father directing from below, the lights from our outside Christmas tree high atop one of the farm's silos could be seen for miles.

Kyle and Travis tied a pulley to the top of the silo and looped a rope through it. At the bottom, Ron tied the tree to one end of the rope and the other end to the bucket of the tractor. As I backed the tractor slowly away from the silo, the tree rose to the top. That was the easy part. I was relieved that the tree was finally up there and I had not been asked to climb. Using the rope and pulley, we sent up a bucket filled with four strings of lights. Then Ron climbed the sixty-five-foot ladder on the side of the silo. He and the boys attached the lights and wired the tree upright to the rails of the catwalk. It was not yet dark when Dad and I connected several extension cords and plugged them into a barn outlet to check for broken or burned-out bulbs.

"Mom," Kyle shouted down, "where are the spare bulbs?"

"In my pocket. Do you need some?"

"Yes," he answered. "Bring them up."

"Who, *me?*"

"Yes, Mom. Come on."

He's got me now, I thought. I should have gone back to the house after the tree was up. I drew a deep breath, reached for the ladder, and slowly placed my foot on the bottom rung. I stopped and looked up; even though there was a cage all around me, my heart was pounding.

"Don't look up, Mom," Travis advised. "Just look at each step as you go. You can do it."

I took several more steps up and looked down. "Don't look down, either," Kyle said.

"What if I fall?" I asked.

"You can't fall," Kyle said. "We need the bulbs if you want this tree to look pretty."

I kept climbing, but to this day, I don't know how I did it. When I reached the top, I peeked up over the edge of the silo. I clung, white-knuckled, with one hand on the top rung. With the other hand, I reached into my pocket for the spare bulbs. Without looking up, I held them up over the edge. "This is the top, up here where we are," Kyle insisted.

"If I go up over the edge, I'll never be able to back off onto the ladder again," I said. "If you want these bulbs, you'll have to come here and get them because I'm not going one more inch."

Without looking sideways, I started my slow descent, exhausted when my feet finally touched the ground again.

"I did it," I said to my father. "My first and last trip up the silo."

After dark we all piled into my father's car. First we drove to the top of The Ridge, and then we went in four different directions to admire the lighted Christmas tree from every possible vantage point. We received so many favorable comments, including those in letters from people we didn't even know, that when the holidays rolled around again, we put up another tree. Ron and Kyle did the job with my mother fretting, unable to watch, and my mother-in-law peering out the window every few minutes, predicting that someone would fall.

The third year, fall work ran into winter and there didn't seem to be time to put up the tree. After Christmas, Ron remarked, "You wouldn't believe how many people have asked why we didn't put a Christmas tree on the silo this year. Guess we'll have to make it a priority for next year."

The fourth year, Kyle and a college fraternity brother launched the tree.

Several days after the lighting, we received a letter from a neighbor, eight-year-old Lynn Keller. She thanked us for putting the tree up again and said how she had missed it the year before.

"How can we not keep on doing it?" Ron asked after reading her letter. "Looks as though it has become a Christmas tradition."

The fifth year wasn't as easy. Kyle had lost his enthusiasm. Ron reminded him that we had started a tradition, so with persuasion and the luck of an unseasonably warm day the first week of December, Kyle gave in. Berna, our second Saint Bernard, watched curiously while we "dressed" the tree on the ground and snugged the branches together with rope. Before launching the tree, we plugged in the lights to test for burned-out bulbs. Berna barked her approval.

When the tree was in place on top of the silo and the lights turned on, I remarked to Kyle how beautiful it looked. "I probably wouldn't have agreed to it," he said, "except Dad says it makes you happy."

It did make me happy, and a lot of other people, too. Maine winters are long, and the tree was a cheerful sight when I headed out to the barn in the early morning darkness of December.

Trudy Chambers Price is a writer and former long-time dairy farmer. This essay was orginally published in her book, The Cows Are Out!

At the Mall with Santa

Joanne Lannin, Maine Sunday Telegram
1993

The spotlights glare. The white beard itches. The red jacket weighs him down. Robert Farwell ignores the discomforts and lets loose with a boisterous "Ho-Ho-Ho" from his perch center stage at the Maine Mall in South Portland.

"I really get into it," says Farwell, forty-three, of his role as mall Santa. "Unfortunately you can't do this twelve months of the year. Otherwise, I would."

Playing Santa brings as much comfort and joy to Farwell's life as it did twenty-five years ago, when he first donned the familiar red suit. He exemplifies the dedication Santas bring to their work year after year, as well as their devotion to keeping the Santa fantasy alive for children.

Farwell is one of four Santas on duty at the Maine Mall this year. By December 24th, they will have listened to the hopes and dreams of seven-thousand to eight-thousand boys and girls from all over Southern Maine.

Farwell also hires himself out as a Santa Claus for children's parties. He "Santas" the annual Coast Guard Base family Christmas gathering in South Portland. He visits area nursery schools and nursing homes.

"Seeing the kids smile. That's the big thing," explains Farwell. "That's what got me started. That's what keeps me going."

Farwell may be a new Santa to the Maine Mall, but he has been playing the part since he was eighteen years old and in the Marine Corps in Memphis, Tennessee.

As he recalls, he was pressed into service to play Santa at a Memphis hospital burn unit. His high school acting experience got him "volunteered," he says. But one particular moment in the burn unit hooked him on playing Old Saint Nick.

"One kid wasn't talking to anyone and he wouldn't smile," Farwell recalls. Farwell didn't try to pressure the boy into talking to him. But as Farwell got up to leave the circle of children, he heard a tiny voice from the back of the room say, "Bye Santa." He knew who it was without even looking.

"That's when I said, 'I like this,'" Farwell recalls. "Just to make someone happy—even for a minute or two—makes me feel good."

Farwell continued to play Santa during his ten-year stint in the Marines, including five and a half years in Japan. There he would walk through the neighborhoods early in the morning on the 24th in his homemade costume.

Farwell, married then to a Japanese woman, fondly recalls sitting his own five-year-old daughter on his knee and asking her what she wanted for Christmas.

"She didn't even know it was me," Farwell says. "That was fun."

Farwell and his wife separated soon after that Christmas, in February 1977. He has kept in touch with his children in Japan, now twenty-one and nineteen, through letters and phone calls. But he hasn't seen them since.

Farwell was born in Portland but moved frequently because his father was in the Coast Guard. He moved back to Maine in 1988. He has been playing Santa Claus for nieces, nephews, and their children ever since delighting, in fooling them the way he once fooled is own daughter.

"He puts on that suit and he *is* Santa," says his second wife, Carol Farwell.

In October, he answered a newspaper ad seeking people to play Santa Claus at the Maine Mall, thinking it would be a good addition to his blossoming Santa business. Farwell's regular job is as a cook at the Cornforth House in Saco.

Mall Santas make $6.50 an hour. Burnett says ten people applied for the four Santa jobs. She was impressed with Farwell's unassuming personality and his method of dealing with shy children.

"You can't force them to sit down," says Farwell of his philosophy. "You just talk to them, find out their name, encourage them. Once they feel relaxed they will come to you. And once they start talking, they won't stop."

One of Farwell's first "customers" on his first night on the job bore out his theory. The little boy hung back and stared wide-eyed at Santa from the edge of the gazebo.

"What's your name?" Farwell asked the toddler in a soft, musical voice. "Would you like to come up here and talk to me?"

The wide-eyed youngster got a nudge from his mother. Then he strode over to Santa and tried to scale his knee. Farwell gently guided the child into the seat beside him on the red sleigh he operates out of.

For some children, sitting beside Santa is less threatening than having to sit on his lap, Farwell explains.

Farwell is not a rotund or imposing figure—he is five feet, nine inches and weighs 190 pounds.

To prepare for his role, Farwell dabs his bushy, salt-and-pepper eyebrows and his moustache with white liquid mascara. Then he dons a stuffing-filled vest that looks like a baseball catcher's chest protector and pulls the drawstring tight around his red velvet pants.

The mall provides all of Santa's gear, including his long, curly white wig and his beard. He straps the wig over his ears and around his head in two places. He anchors the beard over his mustache and around his lips, applying a bit of spirit gum so the sides won't slip.

"You can get a beard made out of yak hair for $175," Farwell says as he fits the bushy beard over his chin. "But it's too expensive to get them dry-cleaned."

Santa's velvet coat with a nylon lining zips up the front. He straps Naugahyde boot-tops over his own ankle high black boots. Then he pulls on his white gloves and admires his profile in the full-length mirror in the middle of the makeshift dressing room that used to be Benoits at the mall.

"While I'm dressing, I'm getting into the spirit of it," Farwell says as he waits for the clock to strike fire. "By the time I'm ready, I'm Santa inside and out."

Indeed, Farwell's cheeks take on a rosy glow as he speaks. When he laughs, his padded belly shakes like the proverbial bowlful of jelly.

According to Burnett, Farwell is one of a rare breed of individuals who can handle the rigors of playing Santa. She usually plans on having to replace at least one Santa each year after the first couple of days on the job.

"The costume is cumbersome and hot," explains Burnett. "Or they discover they don't have the patience they thought they did."

But Farwell considers it a privilege and a responsibility to play Santa Claus to the mall's smallest visitors.

"Whatever comes out of Santa's mouth sticks with them," Farwell says. "The big thing is to listen to them and tell them they are good."

Farwell also throws in the usual advice: brush your teeth, go to bed early, listen to your parents. He also asks them to leave carrots for his reindeer and cookies for him Christmas eve.

As Santa, Farwell gets a first-hand glimpse at how kids' interests have changed over the years. This year girls still want Barbie dolls and accessories. Boys want "Jurassic Park" paraphernalia. Both boys and girls ask for games, computers, and Game Boys. Only one boy so far has asked for a toy gun.

Most of the children who step up to visit Santa at the mall are between three and six, Farwell says. Some seven- and eight-year-olds do come up and talk to him. Whether they still believe in the Santa myth or not, they play along.

Farwell sees no harm in keeping the Santa fantasy alive for children as long as possible—just as his parents did for him.

"I remember when I was eleven, I got up in the middle of the night on Christmas Eve to go to the bathroom," recalls Farwell. "When I came back, the stocking at the end of my bed was full."

"Even after I realized there wasn't a Santa, I felt like there was," he muses. "It's carrying on a tradition that's good for kids. It's pure. It's uplifting. There's nothing negative about it."

The Christmas Cookie-Cutters
Ethel Pochocki
1991

In a dusty back corner of the shelf in a kitchen pantry, an assortment of cookie-cutters lived in a cardboard box tied with twine. Their life was quiet and uneventful. They never went out and had no visitors except for an occasional young spider who, upon investigation, found them of little interest.

Their neighbors—a rabbit cake mold, an Easter basket with pink grass, a grain grinder, a small blue pot for melting wax, a box of rubber canning jar rings—also kept to themselves. You might say that except for the few times a year when they were needed, they also were of little interest.

But once December arrived, the cookie-cutters were brought out from hibernation. The mother of the house, standing on a rickety stool, took the box down and brushed away its blanket of cobwebs, and it became of great importance indeed. The children of the family laid out the cutters lovingly on the kitchen table, greeting each one as an old remembered friend from Christmases past.

Then began the weeks of cookie making, when the kitchen smelled glorious from morn to night of ginger and nutmeg and molasses and vanilla, when flour dusted everything from the children's cheeks to the dog's tail. While a pot of vegetable soup simmered on the stove for supper, the mother and her children made and cut the dough with these special cutters.

They were not all the kind you might expect to use at Christmas. Oh yes, there was the Holy Family and the Fat Santa, a leaping reindeer, the fir tree and snowman, and a sprig of holly. But there were also some very old cutters with handles to press them down which the mother had bought at a rummage sale: a large parrot, a fox with a brush as large as his body, a British soldier with a pointy hat, a trumpet, a Bluebird.

The Bluebird could have been any bird, but the mother called it the Bluebird of Happiness. It was always frosted blue (with almond flavoring) and hung on the topmost branch of the tree near the angel.

There were two gingerbread men, one with a stocking cap and one with heart for a mouth. And there was a gingerbread lady with an apron, a small and large star, a flying angel, and every animal you could imagine—a rabbit, duck, cat, even an elephant and a seal.

Each Christmas, the mother would add a new cutter to the group. One year it was a butterfly. The children didn't want the butterfly.

"Who ever heard of a butterfly at Christmas?" asked one.

"It depends on where you live," said the mother, determined to keep the butterfly.

"Butterflies are for Easter," said a son.

"A stable's too cold for a butterfly," said a daughter.

The mother said nothing and gave the butterfly to the youngest child, who didn't know what a butterfly was and didn't care.

While the children were busy with their cutters, the mother rolled out a honey dough filled with candied fruit and chopped almonds and she cut it into squares the shape of Christmas cards. In the center she pressed the baby Jesus cutter down deep enough to make an impression but not all the way through. Then she put Mary and Joseph on either side of him. A shepherd with a crook stood in one corner, pointing to the star in the other. When the card came out of the oven, the mother covered it with a honey glaze, and when it was cool, wrapped it in a red ribbon and gave it away as a gift.

When the cookies were all baked, the mother whipped up a batch of white vanilla frosting in a large earthenware bowl and then she separated this into seven smaller bowls. She added food coloring to them to make them red and green and blue and yellow and brown, and she flavored them with almond and strawberry and lemon and mint and maple.

In other bowls, which she set in the middle of the table, there were cinnamon red hots and silver shot and chocolate chips and rainbow sprinkles and coconut and, always, raisins for the gingerbread men's buttons.

The children sat around the table amid happy clatter and chatter. Some worked with precise, intense care; others slapped on so much frosting and ornaments, the cookies were too heavy to hang on the tree. *All* were certain they had produced one-of-a kind masterpieces.

On Christmas Eve, the weary floured mother washed the weary floured cutters for the last time and packed them away in the box which would be forgotten for the next eleven months.

So it went for years and years, until the children grew up and moved away and had families of their own and lived too far away to come home for Christmas. The young mother grew old and stopped making cookies because there was no one to eat them. When she died, the children came home one more time to take back with them some small memory of childhood—a crystal vase, a blue and white sugar bowl, a quilt, a clock that chimed, and the cookie cutters.

The eldest daughter took the Holy Family set, and the eldest son picked the gingerbread man and the lady and the fox, and so it went down the line with each of the children taking his favorite. The youngest wanted only the butterfly and the Bluebird of Happiness.

And so the cookie cutters left their old home on the shelf in the pantry and went out into the world to begin new lives making cookies and memories for a new generation of children and, someday, their children.

Ethel Pochocki was a writer and a children's book author who lived in Brooks, Maine. She wrote several award-winning books including Penny for a Hundred. *This essay first appeared in* Echoes *magazine.*

Dear Santa . . .

Kathryn Skelton, Kennebec Journal
2008

They're often addressed to the North Pole or Candy Cane Lane, and requests vary. A Nintendo DS. A skateboard ramp. A job for Dad.

The U.S. Postal Service in Maine has received double the number of letters to Santa this year over last, some sweet, some troubling, some from adults.

Spokesman Tom Rizzo said postal volunteers, subbing as Santa's elves, mailed 1,100 replies last week. Another one-hundred or two-hundred letters have come since.

"We see some wonderful sentiment in them and more than our share of stories of distress," he said Tuesday, the last day letters could be answered and still arrive before Christmas. "Some of them, your imagination can't come up with some of the stories we get this time of year."

Ten postal employees, working on their own time on "Operation Santa," put in hours writing out envelopes and picking from about a half-dozen form letters that start with "Dear little friend" and "Dear my friend."

Kids are thanked for their notes and encouraged to be good, Rizzo said.

Denise Gonneville, of Saco, a financial control and support analyst for the Postal Service, said she opened letters that asked for world peace, money, and Sony PlayStations.

"There was one, he wanted wood to build a skateboard ramp. He wanted nails, he wanted a hammer," she said. "That was cute, I thought."

Christmas Eve at the Chinese Buffet
Maureen Walsh
2013

There are only a few of us here.
It's so quiet except for the sound
Of the silverware,
Hushed voices and Christmas music playing.
There are white lights blinking off and on
In the big window out front.
We are all here for a reason.
Maybe you are new in town
Or your family is fighting
Over something so petty you can't quite remember
What started it all and you don't want to be there
Or maybe you didn't get invited at all.
Maybe your spouse died this past year.
Across from me sits a single woman
With her little boy.
Whatever the reason we are all here together
On this Christmas Eve
Eating chow mein, pork fried rice
And wontons

All Is Calm

At the all you can eat buffet
Before we head out again
Into the dark and silent night.

Lobsters Come Free for the Needy

Edward D. Murphy, Kennebec Journal
2017

No one would ever mistake Noah Ames for Santa Claus.

For one thing, the Matinicus lobsterman is rail-thin and lacks that signature bowl-full-of-jelly belly. He dresses in a sensible parka bundled up against a cold December wind, not a dashing red outfit pulled together with white trim, a black belt, and boots. And Ames' vehicle of choice is a black pickup, not a sleigh, although one suspects that Santa has the edge in roof-landing ability.

Ames does most of his good works on Christmas Eve and, for dozens of Midcoast families, he, like the jolly old elf, shows up once a year to give with no expectation, or desire for anything in return.

And rather than toys, Ames gives away hundreds of crustaceans, doling them out in plastic bags from the back of the pickup rather than Santa's preferred down-the-chimney method of delivery

Ames conducts his giveaway parked out in front of a friend's marine supply store on U.S. Route One in Thomaston.

A simple A-frame sign was plunked into the snow at the edge of the road Sunday: "FREE LOBSTERS TODAY for families truly in need."

One man who saw the sign late Sunday morning pulled in and cautiously walked up to the pickup truck.

"How many do you have to feed?" Ames asked.

"Me, my wife, and four kids," said Freddy Ames (no relation) of Warren.

"Then you'll need a dozen," Noah Ames said, and started tossing the shellfish into a couple of bags aided by his daughter, Nadia, ten.

He handed the bags to Freddy Ames, who said, "What a nice guy" as he turned and walked to his car with his own daughter in tow.

That's Noah Ames' approach: no other questions besides "how many?" No forms to fill out to demonstrate need. If you feel as though you need a hand this holiday, Ames is ready to extend a claw, or two. Plus the tail.

Ames' quest to give away the state's signature product started four years ago, when he felt his children could benefit from a demonstration that Christmas is more than making wish lists and tallying how the "gots" fared against the "wants" on Christmas morning.

So he set out with about a hundred pounds of lobster that he hauled in on his boat, *No Worries*. Other lobstermen and dealers heard of his plan and pitched in totes of lobsters, too. After refusing all offers of money the first few years, last year he accepted donations for a local family with a young girl who has cancer. He continued that this year, as the girl is still battling the disease.

"I didn't count it, but it was quite a bit," he said of the money raised last year.

Rick Whitten said his employer Atwood Lobster, of South Thomaston, is happy to help out with one hundred pounds of the crustacean.

"It's more of a community thing," Whitten said, "and I've never seen anyone taking (undue) advantage of it."

Walter Davis, of Thomaston, said he has stopped in each year Ames has been giving away lobsters. Davis said this year was particularly tough for him and his family, with a half-dozen relatives dying within a few months of one another.

Davis said he's particularly thankful that Ames supplied his holiday meal.

"We've had a lot of things on our minds," he said, "and Christmas dinner wasn't one of them."

On Sunday, it took Ames about an hour to give away four hundred pounds of lobster. He provided one hundred pounds, and the rest came from Atwood Lobster and three other lobstermen.

Ames said he knows what it's like to face hard times, from the normal boom-or-bust life of lobstering to sudden setbacks, such as the time a few months after he began his giveaway, when the *No Worries* sank at its mooring while he was away. He managed to salvage the vessel and get back to lobstering.

But one senses that as much as he likes lobstering, the once-a-year giveaway is what keeps Ames going on those cold February mornings when he heads out to tend his traps.

"Some people (who pick up lobsters) will have tears in their eyes and can't really get their arms around giving lobsters away," he said. "I want to give back to people who are struggling. It's kind of gotten bigger than me. It's a good thing—and the kids are really into it now."

Lewiston-Made Glass Ornaments

Steve Collins, Sun Journal
2018

For more than a decade starting in 1959, a Lewiston factory looked something like a Christmas workshop as it churned out millions of brightly colored ornaments.

Paragon Glass Works, one of the first companies to move into the city's industrial park, produced an astonishing array of glass balls.

Many of them were pretty plain, just colored globes sold for prices that show it's been a while—as little as twenty-nine cents for half a dozen big ones, nineteen cents for a dozen little ones.

Now sought after by Christmas-crazed collectors, they're widely available on eBay and Etsy at prices that make it clear America missed a chance to make a small fortune simply by socking some away in the attic.

Those little cardboard boxes—which cost about $2.50 in today's inflated currency—now sell for as much as $50 apiece, depending on their size and condition.

Some are in teardrop shapes, some carry stenciled scenes. The fancier they look, the more they generally cost.

Consider one box of half a dozen conical glass ornaments produced at least a half century ago at Paragon's Westminster Drive factory: In a box decorated with drawings of ivy and Santa—which saved its largest lettering for "American Made"—there are, among others, a red glass ball with yellow and white stripes, a blue ball with a purple and yellow stripe and a silvery one with a pink and a white stripe.

Paragon competed with larger manufacturers in Germany, Poland, and beyond and, for a time, it was among the bigger glass ornament producers in the United States.

Ernest Paione, an owner of the glassworks, said that early on, foreign competition was tough, but he had faith his company could flourish because ornaments made elsewhere "lacked durability."

By the mid-1970s, though, it couldn't compete with the prices from a growing Christmas industry in Asia, especially with the market for its own products diminishing in America as a fickle public turned away from the seemingly old-fashioned glass balls in favor of the newest and latest.

At that point, Paragon managed to find a new niche, making ever more glass bulbs for automobile headlights and other items that appeared to have a more solid future than holiday ornaments.

Even so, the company closed its doors in 2004, unable to maintain the prices of overseas competitors.

When Paragon opted to move from New Jersey to Maine, it was big news. Even *The New York Times* noted it when the deal was announced in 1958.

The first shipment out from the new factory came in June 1959. It proved such a success that the plant expanded at least twice, in 1962 and 1966.

In December 1959, after its initial forty-thousand-square-foot factory was up and running, Paragon held a big dinner at the old DeWitt hotel in downtown Lewiston to thank Lewiston and state leaders for their hospitality in making its move possible.

Among those in high spirits that night was Gov. Clinton Clauson, a Waterville chiropractor-turned-politician. The sixty-five-year-old Democrat, still in his first year in office, returned to the Blaine House that night and died in his sleep.

In 1967, when a unit in Vietnam wrote to the governor asking if Maine could spare a pine tree so its Christmas could feel like home, Paragon sent along a big box of ornaments with a nine-foot tree that Gov. Kenneth Curtis shipped over to the troops.

One of the women on the receiving end, Ida Colford, later recorded in a book of her experiences that only three of the ornaments arrived broken.

Seeing the the fully decorated Maine tree in Saigon, Colford recalled in an account published in *Women Vietnam Veterans: Our Untold Stories*, "My joy was uncontrollable."

Snowflakes of Christmas

Tristan Noyes
2019

The Christmas season begins in earnest on the Friday after Thanksgiving. I've never taken part in the corporate Black Friday, but the fourth Friday of November always puts me in a merry mood. My family has owned Noyes Flower and Plant Shoppe in Caribou for forty-three years, and for my entire lifetime the last Sunday of November marks our annual open house, a community celebration of the holiday season.

What makes our event so special is not so much the actual open house but rather the process of getting ready for the event. My parents and brother, alongside all of my cousins, aunts, uncles, and my grandmother travel from near and far to be a part of the festivities. One cousin tackles untangling the web of icicle lights and begins hanging them from the ceiling. Another cousin and uncle paint festive borders along each large display window. Others begin assembling and decorating Christmas trees, each bringing their unique style to the task.

Our flower shop's open house is steeped in tradition, not just for our family but also for the city of Caribou itself. Noyes Flower moved to its current location about thirty years ago, but for seventy years before that the building existed as a flower shop under a different owner. The family that owned the building previously bought a series of animatronic elves, reindeer, penguins, and even a polar bear. The life-size figures were originally built and purchased in the 1950s and have graced the windows of our Franklin Street location for nearly sixty years. Each year my father, brother, and I perform amateur reconstructive surgery to help keep the paper-mache bodies upright and in working order. Year after year, elf figures build toys for children, reindeer attend to mending Santa's suit, and a penguin and a polar bear somehow cohabitate in a wintery wonderland in our windows.

From late November to Christmas Day, my father dutifully turns on and off our animated figures, even when the store is closed on Sundays. He makes a special late evening trip from our home so that families can drive through and look with wonder at the beautiful scenes before turning them off for the night. I once had a conversation with a woman who told me that she used to visit the windows of the flower shop with her grandmother when she was just a child. She then introduced me to her own granddaughter who was looking on at the elves with amazement.

Shared traditions help create bonds between family, friends, and community. Traditions ground us and give us a sense of serenity in a world in which change is constant. I have been blessed to have my wife Katherine and my son Bentley join in the Christmas traditions of my childhood. Today, my wife, son, and I live equidistant between our childhood homes in Northern Maine and upstate New York. We alternate between Albany and Caribou each Christmas and Thanksgiving. At first, my wife and I found it a little sad to think of not traveling to our individual parents' homes for the holidays, but it occurred to us that a tradition is still a tradition, even if one doesn't take part in it every year. The tradition may live on in its original form, or it may help influence traditions a new family creates.

Soon after visiting each other's childhood homes, we realized we had overlapping customs. For example, both of our families allowed for the opening of one present on Christmas Eve. Interestingly, Santa always eats a cookie and drinks some eggnog in Albany and Caribou. The best pieces of Christmases past are carried on with us wherever we go. I expect soon, we will begin staying closer to our new Southern Maine home around the holidays, and thus new traditions will be born from the love, comfort, and affection we have been lucky enough to experience in our lives.

When our son was born in December, twelve days before Christmas, we were inspired by the wintry, tradition-filled season when naming him. The name Bentley, a family name on my wife's side, was always near the top our list if we were to have a son. The name was also inspired, in part, by an impromptu visit Katherine and I made to Jericho, Vermont on the way home from visiting friends. In the center of town is a small museum dedicated to the life of Wilson "Snowflake" Bentley. Snowflake Bentley was the first known photographer to capture an image of an individual snowflake. Over a lifetime, he invented and perfected a way to capture snowflakes on black velvet and take pictures of the individual crystals with the help of a bellows camera and microscope. He referred to his snowflakes as "ice flowers" and described them as "tiny miracles of beauty." Snowflake Bentley photographed more than five thousand snowflakes.

Every year, we purchase a pewter Christmas tree ornament designed from an original Snowflake Bentley snow crystal photomicrograph from the Jericho Historical Society. Last year, Bentley was old enough to hang it on the tree himself.

All Is Calm

Snowflake Bentley lamented that when a snowflake melted, its beauty was lost leaving no record of its design—except through his photographs. Thankfully, in contrast, designs of Christmases past can be found in many unexpected places. I can remember distinctly gazing up at the stars as a young child from the backseat of my parents' Chrysler Lebaron on Christmas Eve. My parents asked if I saw the red light from Rudolph's nose. Anyone who has had the privilege to take in the Northern Maine sky on a cold and cloudless night will know the unparalleled majesty of the view. The Milky Way can be seen in all its splendor and a myriad of stars shine in a range of luminosities. It leaves the viewer with the impression that if one stared long and deep enough almost anything could be seen. I am quite certain I saw the red shining of Rudolph's nose that night. Last year, while driving on Christmas Eve, I asked my son if he saw Rudolph's nose in the sky, and as I watched him search, I was quite certain I saw it shining again.

Tristan Noyes is the co-founder of GroMaine Farm and is the Exeutive Director of the Maine Grain Alliance. He lives and writes in South Portland.

Unwrapping
Shawn Callahan
2019

Unwrapping gifts
takes a whole ten minutes
and the rest of the day
is filled with the
reverie of low sun
filtered through
leafless trees.
It snowed a few inches
last week,
so I guess that will do.
The rain that came after
hardened into a sugar slick all
across the lawn. The cold is
durable
but the warmth
rising through the house
is like the redness in my cheeks.
The water and spices
in the pot

All Is Calm

on the woodstove
and the music on the radio
hum in the soft
way of the season.

Bibliography

"A Holiday Wish." (Originally untitled). *Hallowell Weekly Register,* December 12, 1898.

"A Very Roosevelt Christmas (U.S. National Park Service)." National Parks Service. U.S. Department of the Interior. Accessed September 25, 2019. https://www.nps.gov/articles/a-very-roosevelt-christmas.htm.

Barrette, Roy. "Christmas on Naskeag Point." *Down East,* December 1981. Published by permission of David deNagy.

Birch, Alison Wyrley. "Christmas in Castine." *Maine Life,* December 1972. Published by permission of George Frangoulis.

Caldwell, Bill. "A Tree Full of Memories." *Maine Sunday Telegram.* December 24, 1978. Published by permission of MaineToday Media.

Callahan, Shawn. "Unwrapping." 2019.

"Christmas Day." *The Oxford Democrat,* December 24, 1878.

Clark, A Carman. "First Christmas as Maine Homeowners." (Originally titled "Our Neighbors Spread Our Festive Board.") *Maine Life,* December 1973. Published by permission of George Frangoulis.

Cole, John N. "The Glory of Maine at Yuletide." (Originally titled "Maine At Yuletide.") *Down East,* December 1980. Published by permission of Darrah Cole.

Collins, Steve. "Lewiston-Made Glass Ornaments." (Originally titled "Lewiston-Made Glass Ornaments Much Cherished Today.") *Lewiston Sun Journal,* December 25, 2018. Published by permission of MaineToday Media.

Comas, Beatrice. "Sharing Christmas." (Originally untitled). *Maine Life,* December 1974. Published by permission of George Frangoulis.

Conforti, Joseph. "Best-Loved Christmas Traditions Not so Old." *Maine Sunday Telegram,* December 19, 1993.

Cram, Hal. "Christmas on the Lightship." (Originally titled "Christmas Spirit Surrounds The Lightship.") *Sun-Up,* December 1925.

Cyr, Joeseph Donald. "An Acadian Christmas Story." (Originally titled "Noel, 1909.") *Echoes,* 1992. Published by permission of the author.

Davidson, May B. "Christmas in a One-Room School." 2019.

Davis, Doris. "At Christmas." *Maine Life,* December 1971. Published by permission of George Frangoulis.

Ferriss, Lloyd. "Hard Times To Celebrate." *Maine Sunday Telegram*. December 17, 1995.

Furbush, Eva M. "Christmas in Good Old Aroostook." (Originally titled "Christmas Down in Good Old Maine.)" *Maine Woods*, December 12, 1915.

Hamlin, Helen. "Yuletide Cheer and Purple Shirts." *The Pine Cone*, 1945. Published by permission of the Maine Tourism Association.

Hanna, Thomas L. "Wishing for a Merry Christmas," excerpted from *Shoutin' Into the Fog: Growing Up on Maines Ragged Edge*. Islandport Press, 2008.

Jordan, Doris Barbour. "Christmas Reunion." *Maine Life*, December 1972. Published by permission of George Frangoulis.

Klein, Christopher. "When Massachusetts Banned Christmas." History.com. A&E Television Networks, December 22, 2015. https://www.history.com/news/when-massachusetts-banned -christmas.

Lannin, Joanne. "At the Mall with Santa." (Originally titled Santa: From the Back Side of the Beard.") *Maine Sunday Telegram*, December 12, 1993. Published by permission of MaineToday Media.

Libby, Pearl LeBaron. "Christmas Night in Maine." *The Pine Cone,* 1950. Published by permission of The Maine Tourism Association.

Lombard, Lucina H. "Visiting a Lumber Camp for Christmas." (Originally titled "A Christmas Week Visit to a Lumber Camp.") *Sun-Up,* December 1929.

Longfellow, Henry Wadsworth. "Christmas Bells." Poets.org. Academy of American Poets. Accessed September 7, 2019. https://poets.org/poem/christmas-bells.

Lunt, Dean. "An Island Christmas Celebration." 2019.

Lynds, Jen. "Presque Isle Residents Remember Supplying Tree." *Bangor Daily News,* December 9, 2010. https://bangordailynews.com/2010/12/09/news/presque-isle-residents-remember-supplying-national-tree/.

"Maine Tree Shipped to Vietnam." (Originally titled "Maine Christmas Tree Is Being Shipped to Vietnam.") *The Lewiston Daily Sun,* December 11, 1967. Published by permission of MaineToday Media.

Mills, Paul. "How Christmas Became a Holiday in Maine." *Lewiston Sun Journal,* December 22, 2013.

Murphy, Edward D. "Lobsters Come Free for the Needy—No Catch." *Kennebec Journal,* December 26, 2017. Published by permission of MaineToday Media.

Noyes, Tristan. "Snowflakes of Christmas." 2019.

"Pansies for Christmas?" *Rangeley Highlander*, January 1958.

Pochocki, Ethel. "The Christmas Cookie-Cutters." *Echoes,* 1991. Published by permission of Rosemary Marbach.

Price, Trudy Chambers. "Launching a Holiday Tradition," excerpted from *The Cows Are Out!: Two Decades on a Maine Dairy Farm.* Islandport Press, 2004.

Skelton, Kathryn. "Dear Santa . . . " (Originally titled, "Dear Santa . . . Maine Letters Double in 2008.") *Kennebec Journal,* December 24, 2008. Published by permission of MaineToday Media.

Stewart, Katherine W. "Christmas on an Island," *Maine Life,* December 1972. Published by permission of George Frangoulis.

"Winter Comes to Maine," *Maine Seacoast Mission Annual Newsletter*. Published by permission of The Maine Seacoast Mission.

Thompson, Jan. "While the Village Sleeps." *Maine Life,* December 1971. Published by permission of George Frangoulis.

Trott, Rosemary Clifford. "Maine Christmas." *The Pine Cone,* 1948. Published by permission of The Maine Tourism Association.

Walker, Lavina P. "The 'Used-to-Be' Christmas." *Maine Life,* December 1973. Published by permission of George Frangoulis.

Walsh, Maureen. "Christmas Eve at the Chinese Buffet." 2013.

Acknowledgments

Many thanks to the staff at Islandport Press for their expertise and aid in research, design, marketing, and distribution. Thank you also to: The Maine State Library, The Maine Tourism Association, *Down East* magazine, George Frangoulis, Darrah Cole, David deNagy, Rosemary Marbach, The Maine Seacoast Mission, and Lisa DeSisto at MaineToday Media.